Praise for
Packing Light

Ally Vesterfelt is a gifted writer with a pleasant voice who is a joy to spend time with. Joining her on a cross-country journey makes for a delightful and thought-provoking respite. With refreshing honesty, Ally teaches us how to better navigate life and relationships as she navigates the roads of all fifty states.

GARY THOMAS, author of *Sacred Marriage* and *The Sacred Search*

Packing Light is the latest in a long line of rich and lovely travel memoirs that make the world bigger, that make us long for the open road, and that ask us to consider the important and universal themes of faith, fear, comfort, friendship, love, and what to pack. For any young traveler, literal and otherwise, Ally has given us a gem.

SHAUNA NIEQUIST, author of *Cold Tangerines, Bittersweet,* and *Bread & Wine*

This is a good one, an important book for those who are restless. We all have questions, and some brave souls turn to the call of the open road for answers. Thanks, Ally, for sharing your journey with us. I couldn't stop reading.

JEFF GOINS, author of *Wrecked: When a Broken World
*Slams into Your Comfortable Life***

Allison Vesterfelt has written a wonderfully provocative book about changing your life. For a long time she was plagued by a thought, "could I live life where nothing held me back?" It would mean leaving a lot behind. But the dream grew inside her until one day she sold everything and, packing lightly, took off for the open road and a life full of possibilities.

If, like her, you're tired of the complicated life you're living, you'll want to read *Packing Light* and consider following her example. In simplicity and abandon, Vesterfelt found the purpose she longed for. It's a great story and a lesson I found invigorating to my spirit.

SETH BARNES, CEO Adventures in Missions

I've known Ally since we were kids. She's everything you want in a writer: smart, funny, honest, flawed, strong, passionate, and after Jesus' kingdom vision. To a generation that's dying for adventure but scared to death of failure, *Packing Light* comes as a much needed kick out the front door. You might read this book on your couch, but you won't stay there.

JOHN MARK COMER, pastor for teaching and vision at Solid Rock:
a Jesus church in Portland, Oregon

Allison Vesterfelt is one of the best emerging writers to come along in years. Her words slip into the next ones in a way that makes reading a delight. And then there's the story she tells. From page one, you feel drawn in, as if you were having coffee together, sharing personal confessions with a friend. This book will occupy a permanent space in your library.

BEN ARMENT, creator of STORY and Dream Year

Ally did what so many of us have dreamed of doing at some point. Her journey was adventurous and life-changing. I vicariously joined in the journey as I read along. *Packing Light* is heartfelt and insightful, and you should read it now!

ALLI WORTHINGTON, entrepreneur, business coach and consultant, speaker and fan of all things digital

Ally tells her story with such grace, honesty, and humor that we can't help but get caught up in her journey with her. Her trip may be unique to her, but the lessons she learned are universal. *Packing Light* is a book for anyone longing to go after that "something missing" in their own lives.

JUSTIN LATHROP, blogger and cofounder of Some Company

Packing Light makes you want to get out large scissors and cut the strings holding you back. Packing your bags with boldness, wisdom, and fresh perspectives, this book bravely takes you on a journey of themes so relevant to people of this day and age. At times you feel like you are truly in her shoes—with her lessons you learn your own, with her broken expectations you break yours, with her found freedom you yourself feel refreshed.

SARAH DUBBELDAM, editor in chief of *Darling* magazine

packing light

thoughts on living life with less baggage

Allison Vesterfelt

MOODY PUBLISHERS
CHICAGO

All Scripture quotations, unless otherwise indicated, are taken from the Holy Bible, New International Version®, NIV®. Copyright © 1973, 1978, 1984 by Biblica, Inc.™ Used by permission of Zondervan. All rights reserved worldwide. www.zondervan.com. The "NIV" and "New International Version" are trademarks registered in the United States Patent and Trademark Office by Biblica, Inc.™

Published in association with the literary agency of Darrell Vesterfelt.

This is a work of nonfiction. Though names, places, and other identifers may be altered to protect the privacy of those involved, the events and thematic elements faithfully represent the author's experiences, context, and insights gleaned.

Edited by Stephanie S. Smith of (In)dialogue Communications
Interior design: Design Corps
Cover design: Gilbert & Carlson Design, LLC dba Gearbox
Cover image: Veer/GoodMood Photo #4647420
Author photo: Lucas Botz Photography

Library of Congress Cataloging-in-Publication Data

Vesterfelt, Allison.
    Packing light : thoughts on living life with less baggage / Allison Vesterfelt.
        pages cm
    ISBN 978-0-8024-0729-0
    1. Conduct of life. 2. Simplicity. I. Title.
    BJ1589.V47 2013
    248.4—dc23
                            2013016093

We hope you enjoy this book from Moody Publishers. Our goal is to provide high-quality, thought-provoking books and products that connect truth to your real needs and challenges. For more information on other books and products written and produced from a biblical perspective, go to www.moodypublishers.com or write to:

Moody Publishers
820 N. LaSalle Boulevard
Chicago, IL 60610

3 5 7 9 10 8 6 4 2

Printed in the United States of America

To all those who shared their couches,
their comforters, and their coffee with us.
We couldn't have done it without you.

And to my husband, my number one guy,
without whom there would be no book, thanks
for being the climax of my packing light story.

Contents

Foreword

MY FAVORITE PART OF the circus lasts less than a second. It's the part where the trapeze artist is flying through the air between the swinging ropes. He has let go of one and is reaching for the other.

When I see it happen, I always wonder about the first time he did it. What did it feel like the first time he let go of the rope? He'd swung back and forth a million times, getting the timing right, watching the other rope swing toward and then away, imagining what it would be like to one day let go.

And then, he did it. And in that millisecond all the unspoken emotions swelled up in him, all the stuff about risk and identity and work and the hope he was doing it right. There is so much about life captured in that set of emotions.

The thing is, though, you watch the guy now and he swings across the arena with ease.

I think life is like that. The older we get, the more we swing through our transitions with maturity and grace. But do you remember the first time? Do you remember going off to college? Your first crush? Your first job interview? Do you remember your first road trip? The first time you got up in front of a crowd to read a poem or play a song?

That's the stuff. Certainly those memories quickly get replaced with getting married and having kids and the chapters in life that make it truly beautiful, but there are times I still miss the thrill of those first big risks, when what seem like small events felt enormous and frightening. Leaving. Loving. Fighting. Throwing away stuff. Praying for gas money.

Packing Light is a book about the millisecond of feeling that happened when Allison Vesterfelt let go of one rope and reached out for the other.

Ally has been a friend now for some time. I love her and her husband. It was fun to read about who she was before we met, though, knowing she nailed the landing. That said, as grateful as I am she caught the other rope, I'm even more grateful she let go of the first one.

My favorite part of the circus is my favorite part of life. Here's 250 pages describing it.

—Donald Miller
New York Times bestselling author of *Blue Like Jazz*

You'll never meet a traveler who,
after five trips, brags: "Every year I pack heavier."
The measure of a good traveler is
how light he or she travels.

RICK STEVES

Introduction

where the journey begins

I GREW UP IN Portland, Oregon. That's the first thing I always tell people about myself. It might seem like such a small thing to tell someone meeting you for the first time, but in my case it is not small, and I doubt it is in yours, either. Places are not just places. The place you start your journey is your anchor, the filter through which you process every single stop along the way. Our places shape us and teach us until, before we know it, we do not just live in a place. It lives inside of us.

The second thing I would tell someone if they asked me is that I'm a Christian. I grew up in a conservative Christian home with parents who were missionaries, at least until my dad went back to school to get his doctorate. My mom is exuberant in her love for Jesus. Wherever she goes, she oozes with "PTLs" (Praise the Lord) and Bible verses and invitations to church. My dad, on the other hand, has always stood back, quiet and thoughtful, chewing on belief, letting it fully digest.

This is where I began, somewhere between these two worlds. Somewhere between the careful, conservative upbringing of Christian parents, and the wild, thought-provoking world of the Pacific Northwest. Somewhere between the boisterous faith of my mother and the thoughtful consideration of my dad. This was my starting point.

Your starting point matters when you go on a trip. It is your only frame of reference for what to bring, and what to leave behind. It is your foundation, your beginning. If, along the way, you realize you've been heading the wrong direction, you might change your trajectory, but you can't change where you started. You have to leave home to go on a journey, but you can't leave home without having a home. Portland was that home for me.

Growing up Christian in Portland was its own challenge. The city values individuality and self-expression, a fact you wouldn't miss if you walked the streets on any given day. You would see people of all different stripes, expressing themselves in every imaginable way. You would see the full spectrum from "normal" to "crazy." You would see business suits and Santa suits. There would be dresses with running shoes, and tutus on grown women. We don't try to hide our strangeness from others. In fact, we're really proud of it. We believe it makes us special. Just look at the "Keep Portland Weird" stickers and billboards all over the city.

Strangely enough, the one individual decision that seems to be under scrutiny in Portland is the decision to be a Christian. Although I can see why—Christianity as a whole hasn't exactly gained a reputation for being open-minded, and I can see how the church stands as a threat to personal freedom. But as a result, I grew up knowing faith wasn't something I could talk about safely outside of the church building. My church taught "evangelism," and I knew I wasn't supposed to hide my lamp under a bushel, or something like that, but I learned the quickest way to lose friends was to talk about Jesus, church, or my parents' job as missionaries to my friends at school.

It's cool to be smart in Portland. It's cool to be politically active, to read books, to use big words like "socially constructed realities." It's important to think for yourself, resisting anything that might be considered "corporate" or controlling or "the man." Perhaps this part of my city's heritage contributed to why I grew up with a hunger to try to experience things for myself and make my own decisions. This sometimes got me into trouble in church, but it rarely stopped me. I learned at a young age that one way to cope with the tension was to lie—especially about books, movies, and music. At school I would laugh at quotes from movies I had never seen, feign excitement over albums I had never listened to, and fake familiarity with magazines I wasn't allowed to read. At church, I would pretend like I hadn't snuck over to my friend Marilynn's house to watch *Jerry Maguire* with her and the other popular girls after school.

I was stuck between two worlds. I loved them both. I didn't always agree with everything other Christians said or did, but I knew I loved Jesus and I wanted to be a part of the huge, messy, beautiful story being written. And for all Portland's quirks, I would defend it to my dying breath.

To outsiders, I defended its people, who I saw as eclectic and beautiful, even when they fell outside of the church's understanding of "acceptable behavior." I defended the weather, explaining to those who had never been that, although it rained nine months out of the year, it was really just a light drizzle. I explained how we were not just a bunch of tree-huggers. We cared about the environment. We wanted to protect and stay connected to the earth God had given us. And they're *not* Birkenstocks, for the last time. They're Chacos, and they're comfortable.

At the same time, I found myself tempted to defend the church to a city that wasn't always receptive to Christianity. I vowed to be the Christian who was nice to people, and tipped well, and didn't stand around holding a sign that said, "God hates fags." The God I knew didn't hate anyone, and I was desperate for people to know it.

One summer I worked at a restaurant with several atheists. One of them got word I was a Christian and invited me over to have a beer with some of his friends (later, I secretly pictured him calling those people saying, "You guys, you have to come over tonight! I found one! A real, live Christian!"). We spent the night sitting in a circle on his front porch, sipping our microbrews talking about God. They asked me a hundred questions, and I said, "I don't know," about a hundred times. At the end of the night, my friend walked me to the door and said, resolutely, "Thanks for coming over. I've never met a Christian who would have a beer with me." Then he added, "Or say, *I don't know.*"

That is the place I lived, where I always tried to bridge the gap.

The collision of church and culture left me confused in many ways, the kind of confusion that is most disorienting because I didn't know it was happening. There was the discussion of bodies, for example, which in the wider culture went something like this: *Your body is a temple. You should worship it, be nice to it, take care of it, always make sure it is beautiful above all else.* As a city, this meant yoga classes and Pilates classes, running, and a careful consideration of everything you put in your mouth. It meant organic, whole foods, vegan, vegetarian, and gluten-free. It meant acupuncture over pills and prescriptions.

The conversation in the church, of course, sounded a little different. It went something like this: *Your body is a temple. It is eternal, and not your own. You should cover it up, keep it from harm, and save it for the sacred and special.* This meant virginity talks and letters to my future husband and arguments about homosexuality, heaven, and hell.

The two conversations were disparate enough that I could see the disagreement, but just similar enough that the hostility seemed very confusing. I wanted people in the church to see the value of the people in Portland, and the people in Portland to see the value of the church. And I wanted to know why you had to pick one side or the other.

Yet despite the conflict between the church and the wider culture in Portland, the two influenced each other. They danced together, at least in my life, teaching each other things, picking up habits from one another, and sayings, like two people, the odd couple, living in the same house. It was an ever-swirling conversation of art and politics and music and God and taco carts.

I say all this not to promote myself or where I'm from, but to show you how much baggage I was carrying without even realizing it. Baggage is like that. You pick it up one piece at a time, and it grows heavy over time, so you hardly even realize you're carrying it.

And the only way we know we're holding it is if we go somewhere. As long as we stay stationary, we'll never realize how full our arms, and our suitcases, really are. But when we decide to go somewhere, we discover we can't take it with us.

This is my story of my baggage and my trip. It isn't your story—though you no doubt have one just as full of twists and turns and pain and wonder. But I hope that as you read it, you will see yourself in it. We are all carrying baggage—things we've picked up at home, past experiences, expectations for what's ahead. It might look different than mine, but it weighs you down just the same. I hope it will encourage you to go on a trip.

1

plan a trip

"Our battered suitcases were piled on the sidewalk again; we had longer ways to go. But no matter, the road is life."
JACK KEROUAC

IT ALL STARTED WITH a wedding. So many good stories do. There was a church, a big white dress, a bunch of bridesmaids, and then there was me. Getting ready alone. Driving to the ceremony alone. Sitting in the pew inches from friends, but still very much alone.

It wasn't the going alone part that bothered me. That much I had done at least a dozen times before. It was this strange feeling I was carrying with me—that may or may not have had anything to do with the wedding. It was a restlessness, a confusion, a tension. I was twenty-six years old, with a graduate degree under my belt and a job as a middle-school English teacher to show for it. This is what I had worked and waited for—what I had hoped would be the culmination of all my school loans, studying, and internships. This was supposed to be the climax—but it didn't feel like that. It felt like something was missing.

On the outside at least, many other things were coming together. I had been approved for a home loan, first of all. There was this beautiful condo in northwest Portland that had caught my eye, and I had decided to just see if I could buy it. It was quaint and small, barely big enough for just me, but it was walking distance to restaurants and boutiques and close to the highway I took to get to work. It was in the quiet part of the neighborhood, a few blocks from the commotion—just the way I liked it. And I had friends who lived within biking distance. I pictured dinner parties and dropping by just to say "hi" and calling at the last minute to see if we all wanted to grab dinner on one of Portland's perfect summer nights. I couldn't imagine anything better. And according to the broker I had talked to, I could afford it.

But every time I thought about taking the leap, something inside me resisted. It just didn't seem right. I didn't want to buy a house all by myself.

My friend Erica, on the other hand, wouldn't have to.

She looked beautiful as she made her way down the aisle to instrumental music, dragging tiny rose petals in her train trailing behind her. I was happy for her—I really was. I didn't feel the dull ache of jealousy I had in the past watching wedding after wedding.

But I felt the tiniest twinge of sadness. She was about to cross the threshold into married life—a line I wasn't sure I would ever cross—and things would never be the same. If I had learned anything in my twenty-six years, I had learned that.

Six years ago, it had happened to me for the first time, although there had been many others since. My college roommate got married. Before the wedding, we did everything together—eating together, doing homework together, watching afternoon reruns of *Dawson's Creek* together, sitting awake together in a sterile hospital room as her dad slowly faded away from life, until the pressing questions about God and life and what happens on the other side quietly subsided. But now, we didn't do anything together. She did all these things with her husband. Which meant I did everything alone. Including attend her wedding.

It was fine. I wasn't mad about it or anything. That's what you're supposed to do when you get married, right? You're supposed to do stuff with your husband. That's what getting married is all about, isn't it—the fact that you don't have to do stuff alone anymore. It's just that after several years of finding friends and getting attached to those friends, only to then watch them get married and lose them, you learn not to get too attached to anyone.

You don't disengage from friendships or give up on them forever, you just learn that they're more temporary than you once thought they were. You swear to yourself that you'll never be that way when you get married—but you know in your heart that the truth is, you probably will be—so you question if you even want to get married anyway. You learn the really important coping mechanism to single life: to be independent and take care of yourself. You learn to make the most about being alone.

That's exactly what I was thinking about as I watched Erica float down the aisle that day. I was thinking about how much I liked my single life, about how I didn't much mind being alone. I thought about how I could go anywhere I wanted to go, whenever I wanted to go there, and how I didn't have to ask permission before I spent money. I thought about how I could change jobs whenever I wanted, or move to a different part of town, or even a different city. I thought about how I was able to invest in my career, and my friendships, and my hobbies.

I wasn't just making this stuff up. I really felt it.

But as I sat in the pew and quietly watched Erica give her life to the man who stood in front of her, I couldn't get rid of this nagging question in the back of my mind: *What was I supposed to give my life to?*

After the ceremony ended, I drove carefully through the rainy November night to the reception, where cute little finger food options were offered on trays in the perfectly appointed ballroom. I helped myself to a glass of wine and planted myself on a couch off to the side, where I could watch the party unfold from a distance. That is how I liked it. Life on the sidelines. Low risk. Low-key. And really entertaining.

It was a strategy I had developed a long time ago, without putting much thought into it. Since I didn't really love big crowds, any time I went to an event where I had to be in a room full of people, I would position myself on the fringe of the room. Preferably, I could have my back against an outside wall and plant myself there for the duration of the evening. Usually, I would bring some food with me—rations to sustain me for the night—and also something to make me look like I was busy. Sometimes I would carry a book in my purse; sometimes I would use my phone. Sometimes I would scribble notes in a little notebook.

The benefit of this strategy was that I got to keep tabs on everybody. I got to watch the token single guy make a fool of himself with every single girl in the room, introducing himself and recycling the same cheesy jokes over and over again. I got to watch the "important" people in the room try to downplay their importance, and everyone else try to prove how "important" they were. I could make fun of people (secretly, of course, in my head) for telling jokes that tanked, or for going in for a handshake while the other person went in for a hug—or the most tragic, mistaking a high five for a hug request. That was the worst.

The other benefit of my strategic sidelining, I'll admit, is that no one could approach me from behind. This way, I was never shocked by anything. If someone wanted to talk to me, they could approach me from the front, like a civilized partygoer. I'm not sure why that was such a big deal to me. I think there must have been one too many tragic "cover-your-eyes-from-behind" experiences buried in my high-school psyche. I could keep track of who was friends with who, and who appeared to be nice, and who appeared to be no fun at all.

From my spot on the wall I could watch the whole party unfold. It was like charting the course of the story, with all of its characters, all sticky and messy and wonderful.

And if someone did want to talk to me, they knew where to find me. After all, I didn't move for the entire party. I wasn't really hard to track down. When they came to talk to me, I would be there—ready, with my food prop in place and my tone of voice prepared to meet them enthusiastically (if they were "that" type) or intellectually (because I overheard them talking about the Pleistocene era, and I googled it so I could know what it was).

This was the way to do a party, if you asked me.

I watched my friend Sharaya, one of the bridesmaids, throw her head back in laughter talking to three guys, none of whom I had seen before. Her blonde hair was pinned in a loose up-do and her dress curved flatteringly around her figure. I had watched her at church before, leading worship from stage, and thought about how beautiful she was, how stylishly put together. But tonight, with her high heels and perfectly applied lipstick, she looked more elegant than ever.

I was jealous of people like that, if I'm being honest with you—people who always looked elegant even when they were in the mess of the party, people who seemed to float through life laughing and making the most out of everything.

The problem was, it was impossible to hate her. She was like a cartoon character, always smiling and giggling and swooping in and out of scene after scene with another exciting story. Sharaya was the type of girl who would disappear and show up a few days later, saying she just couldn't help but take a quick trip to Los Angeles or Australia. Whatever. She was always going on flying trips or sailing trips or horseback-riding trips. I could never figure out where she met all these people with horses or boats or airplanes. I wondered if maybe she could introduce me to some of them.

One time she was dropped off at a Sunday night church service gripping a bag full of her belongings. It all happened so quickly that I swear the car didn't even stop all the way as she tumbled out the door. "Hello everyone," she seemed to say as she sashayed into the crowd. "I'm sorry I'm late," she told us, even though she wasn't late at all. "I got tied up wakeboarding." I couldn't figure it out. Her clothes weren't wet or wrinkled in the slightest. Her skin was flawlessly tanned so that she glowed a little, almost like she was wearing makeup, but there were no signs of mascara or eyeliner smudges under her eyes. Her hair was air-dried in this whimsical little ponytail that looked so perfect as it bounced on top of her head.

Sharaya and I couldn't have possibly been more different. We looked different, first of all. She was blonde, petite, and impossibly athletic. Every time I saw her, I wondered what her secret was to keeping her arms so toned. I, on the other hand, was tall with long, dark hair and equally long, gangly limbs. I had recently taken up running, as was the trend in Portland at the time, but I didn't dare play group sports or do any activity where someone could accuse me of throwing like a girl (because I did).

Sharaya was also free-spirited and fun, always making interesting conversation and smiling, even when she was the brunt of the joke. I was quieter—more serious but more imaginative too, the kind of girl who spends her weekends reading and organizing her closet.

And for my whole life, I had dreamed of being a writer.

When she walked up to me that night at the wedding, I should have known it would change my life forever.

The party was starting to pick up a bit. Everyone had eaten some food and the groom's younger brother had taken over the microphone, so just when things were starting to get interesting, Sharaya came and sat by me.

"Hey!" She greeted me warmly. "Want to come dance?" She might as well have been glowing.

"I don't think so . . ." I told her.

"Come on!" she urged. "It'll be fun!"

I told her I wasn't much of a dancer and, besides, if I came to dance I would have to put down my glass of wine, and I wasn't sure I was willing to make that trade right now.

"Fair enough," she conceded.

Outside the party, the city of Portland looked beautiful, even with the gentle haze of rain settling over it. It had an eerie quality to it—gentle and melancholy. We looked west, toward the river. That's when I saw the billboard.

"I climbed up there once," I said, pointing to the billboard in the distance.

I hadn't planned to say it, but we were sitting there, and I wasn't sure what else to say, so it just popped out. This is why I stay on the perimeter of parties like this. I wasn't trying to impress her, at least not consciously, but I think that somewhere deep inside of me my subconscious was saying, "Hey, I might not have friends with airplanes, and I might not look like a hair model after wakeboarding, but my life is exciting too."

"Really?" she asked. "For what?"

"A friend made me do it," I said, and immediately regretted it, because it retracted any cool points I may have just earned. She looked at me expectantly.

"I mean, a friend and I climbed up there together," I corrected myself. "You can see the whole city."

She seemed interested.

"He and I looked out at the view and talked about life now and dreams we had for life someday," I told her. She raised her eyebrows a little.

"It's his job," I clarified. "Besides, he's not my type. He's always jet-setting off to other countries to go on skiing trips or jump out of airplanes. Actually, come to think of it, you two would make a great couple," I told her. "I should introduce you."

The newlyweds were on stage now, starting their first dance together.

"What would you do with your life if you didn't have to worry about money?" I said, after a minute. "That's the question he asked me while we were sitting up there."

"And?" Sharaya asked.

"It made me mad," I said, laughing a little. "He was trying to inspire me, but instead it just made me angry." I took another sip of wine.

"Why?"

"Because I was working a restaurant job at the time, trying to pay my way through graduate school. And not everyone has the luxury of living the way he lives. I don't know where he gets all of his money."

"Did you ever answer his question?" Sharaya asked.

"Yeah, I told him that if I really didn't have to worry about paying my bills—which I *do* by the way, everyone does—I would drive across the country and write a book about it." I shrugged. "But normal people don't get to just quit their lives and go on road trips." I ran my hands across the royal blue velvet couch, watching the way it changed colors depending on the direction of the nap.

"Where would you go?" she asked.

"Everywhere. All fifty states."

Outside, lights flashed, and we watched as the traffic stopped so the road could lift and a boat could pass under the Steel Bridge.

"You know, I've always wanted to travel across the country," she said.

"Really? What would you do?"

"Play music."

It didn't surprise me. She had a beautiful voice. I thought so every time I heard her sing at church. I just didn't know, until she told me, that she'd written a few songs of her own and was working to record her first album.

"It's just an EP," she said.

"Well, I don't even know what that is," I said. "So you've got me beat."

Over the next few hours Sharaya convinced me to get up from my seat and get into the fray of the party. I had a good time, I'll admit, watching the bride and groom shove cake into each other's mouths and meeting all of Sharaya's friends. She even got me to dance for a little bit.

But she wasn't quite done prodding me out of my comfort zone. At the end of the evening, when I was finally fishing my keys out of my purse, she suddenly asked, "So when are we going to go on that road trip?"

It was midnight, and the couple had just left. We'd blown bubbles at them as they drove away, and I couldn't believe I had stayed this late. I laughed a little and shook my head. I was proud of myself for getting off the couch, but a road trip? That wasn't going to happen.

It was a nice thought, I told her, but not in the slightest bit realistic. It would cost too much, first of all—between food, lodging, gas, and then anything unexpected like the car breaking down or someone getting sick. You had to plan for things like that. Plus, we both had jobs and apartments, and I had a roommate who was counting on me to pay rent each month. Even if we were to move out of our apartments, or quit our jobs, what would we do with all of our stuff? After all, I had worked really hard to get my job. Hadn't she? Four years of undergraduate. Two-and-a-half of graduate school. Internships. School loans. Sweat and sleepless nights and tears. Finally, I had the job I had worked for. What was I going to do, just quit? What would my parents say? What would our friends think?

"I'm twenty-six," I told her. "I don't think it's wise to be planning cross-country road trips."

"Listen, Ally," she said, looking directly at me. "I've been writing more music lately and wanting to play more shows in our area. I think this would be a great way to motivate myself to do that. And sure, you have a good job. So do I. But is this really what you want to do with the rest of your life? Or do you want to write a book? If we went on a road trip, you could write while we traveled. You could even keep a blog, and by the end of it, I think you might have your book. We could sell CDs along the way. We'd make some money that way, and we could order T-shirts too, and collect tips at each of my shows."

It seemed she had a way out for every objection I could come up with.

"We could stay with people we know, Ally. Think about it. We would ask people to take us in for a night—just one night. That wouldn't be that big of a deal, would it? And all the stuff that's in our apartments—I think if we sold all of that stuff, we could probably make enough money to cover us for a while. Let's get serious, do you really want a couch and a couple of dressers to keep you from what could be the best experience of your life?"

I didn't want to agree with her. I wanted to get mad and tell her she was ridiculous, but something about the sound of her voice and the sincerity of her offer made it impossible for me to do that. Her passion just made everything she was saying sound feasible and exciting. I didn't want to believe it was, but as I climbed in my car I heard myself tell her I would think about it. Not that I would go—but that it was open for discussion and that we would talk about it more tomorrow.

That's the thing with ideas. They start small, somewhere inside of you, and nothing will happen with them until you finally speak them out loud. We hold on to ideas for years sometimes, because we think they're meaningless, or impossible, or that people will laugh at us when we tell them. Or, maybe we hold on to them because we forget we even had them in the first place. But then, if we're lucky, we have a temporary blip in judgment—brought about by the whimsy of a wedding or an extra glass of wine—and we just let the words come tumbling out.

2

pack your bags

"Twenty years from now you will be more disappointed by the things you didn't do than by the ones you did do. So throw off the bowlines, sail away from the safe harbor. Catch the trade winds in your sails. Explore. Dream. Discover."

MARK TWAIN

BEFORE MY WEDDING RUN-IN with Sharaya, I had my routine pretty much down. On weekdays, my alarm would go off at five, and I would go for a run. When I returned, I would make coffee in my French press and read my Bible while I watched the sun come up. Then I would shower, eat breakfast, pack my lunch, and make the twenty-four minute drive to my school.

I taught six forty-five-minute periods during the day—six of seven, total—which meant I had one prep period and a lunch break. All six were English classes, but two were beginning, two were intermediate, and the other two were for advanced middle school kids. Monday during my prep period I would work on lesson plans for the remainder of the week, Tuesday I would make any photocopies I needed, Wednesday I would grade papers, Thursday I would make parent phone calls, and Friday I would finish whatever I had missed on the previous days. Organization was the only way I made it through each day.

The final bell rang at 3:55 p.m. and I would hold the door open while eighth graders rushed out to their buses. Then, I would drive home, or to whatever activity I had planned that day. Monday was "House Church" (our church's version of small group); Tuesdays I would sometimes meet my dad for dinner between his clients; Wednesdays were dinner parties with friends or happy hour in the Pearl District; and Thursdays I always went home because I was always tired.

"Home" was a spacious apartment just over the West Hills in Portland where I lived with my friend Rebecca. It was outside of the city but not quite to the suburbs, and surrounded by running trails we loved. It wasn't fancy, but we had it decorated to our liking and had come up with a sort of rhythm together. Not every roommate is like this, but we were more friends than roommates.

We both loved to cook and to read, and we both ordered our lives in such a way that was reliable and constant. We didn't own a TV, although sometimes we would watch old reruns on her desktop computer, which sat on a desk in our spacious living room. The only other piece of furniture in the room was a purple couch that was more comfortable than it was aesthetic.

As for the rest of the room, we filled it with Denise Austin's Body Burn yoga DVD exercises, or elaborate indoor picnics. Or sometimes we would create our own beauty salon, borrowing giant Tupperware containers from the kitchen and filling them with bath salts and hot water. We'd light candles and put on face masks and talk to each other with our feet submerged in their own private baths. Someone would say something funny and we would laugh until we fell over, still trying to keep our feet covered in their salted water.

Our home wasn't perfectly put together, but it was ours. Between the two of us, most of what we needed was in the kitchen, and our separate bedrooms were arranged just how we liked them. On weekends, between running, grocery shopping, going to church, and visiting with our families, we would take shopping trips to look for things we still felt like we were missing. But by Monday mornings, we were always back to our schedules again.

Usually, we were in bed by nine. Not every day, but most days. It didn't seem to matter what we were doing—reading a book, watching a movie, or out to dinner with friends—whatever was going on, around nine, I would feel my body tell me that it was time to go to sleep. I would look to Rebecca, and she would nod in agreement. We would quietly disengage and do what we needed to do in order to head toward bed.

It was so comfortable, the life I was living. It wasn't perfect, but it was lovely, which is why I felt so guilty for wondering if it was enough. It's why I talked myself out of feeling I was missing something. It's also why I felt sick inside at the thought of giving it up.

MAKING LISTS

Powell's Bookstore sits on the corner of 10th and Burnside in Portland's Pearl District, and the three-story building covers an entire city block. It's divided into rooms, which are delineated by colors, so if you want to find books on psychology you'll go to the red room on the second floor. If you want to find cookbooks, you'll go to the orange room on the bottom floor, and if you want to look at the collection of rare manuscripts, you'll have to climb all the way to the third floor.

Sharaya lived on 10th and Northrup—about ten blocks from Powell's in a high-rise apartment that overlooked the city. The Pearl District is ordered alphanumerically, so if you don't know exactly where you are, or how to get somewhere, you can always find your way if you know your cross street. The number streets go in order, and each runs North-South. The letter streets go in alphabetical order—Davis, Everett, Flanders, Glisan—and run East-West. So if you're on 10th and Lovejoy and trying to go to 10th and Burnside, you know that Burnside (the "B" street) is ten blocks away from where you are. In Portland, that's perfect walking distance. I loved the Pearl District for how predictable it was. No surprises. Just consistency. It was easy to navigate, easy to manage, every time.

I made my way to Sharaya's apartment on the streetcar, even though it was raining. She had invited me over to drink coffee and talk about "our trip." She kept saying it that way—"our trip"—as if it was actually going to happen. I kept thinking I was going to have to break it to her, gently, that this whole thing wasn't very likely.

At the same time I couldn't help but wonder—could we make it work? It couldn't hurt to talk about it, could it? No, I shook my head to myself. This whole thing was impossible and probably irresponsible too. I thought about the budget I had put together, thanks to Dave Ramsey, and how much I was paying toward my school loans each month. Yes, it was official. I was going to have to tell Sharaya—today—that there was no way we could afford to do this. I braced myself for the conversation and climbed off the streetcar on 10th and Lovejoy, pulling up my hood for the last two blocks to her apartment.

I had hardly taken a sip of my coffee when she dove right in.

"Let's make a list," Sharaya said. She was at the kitchen table, curled up in the chair. I sat on the couch, leaning in.

"What kind of a list?"

"A list of things that would have to happen if we were going to go on our trip."

"Sharaya, we need to talk about this."

"Look, Ally. I know you're really skeptical about this whole thing, and that's okay. I get it. But let's just dream for a minute. Here's all I'm asking. We each make a list of the things that would have to happen if we were going to do a trip like this. Then, when the lists are done, we'll take a look and see if the tasks look reasonable. If they do, we try to do them; if they don't, we give up. Easy enough, right?"

I couldn't argue with that.

"Here's my list," she continued. I could see she'd already put a great deal of thought into this. "First, I would have to finalize my EP and book a few local shows."

I nodded again.

"If I can book some local shows, that's a pretty good indication I'll be able to book shows other places, and I need to practice playing in front of people."

"You play in front of people practically every Sunday."

"Trust me, it's not the same," she said.

She read me the rest of her list, which included finding a renter for her condo, selling her car, and telling her dad, who she predicted was not going to be happy about the idea. This was just a preliminary list, she explained. It didn't need to include things like quitting our jobs, selling all of our stuff, or raising the thousands of dollars we would need to fund our trip.

"Keep it small for now," she kept saying. "We're not committing to anything; we're just researching."

Research. I liked research. I could handle that.

"What about your list?" she asked even though I was really hoping she wouldn't. I took a deep breath.

"First, I'd have to defer my school loans," I said, gripping my orange coffee mug with both hands. I paused. Sharaya wrote it down. "My car is paid off, so I guess we could take it with us, but I'd have to have a mechanic check to make sure it's up for a long trip." I held the cup in front of my face so I could breathe in the steam as it floated upward. "And I would have to ask Rebecca if it's okay if I'm gone for six months." I felt my stomach flip when I said the words out loud.

"That's good."

I watched as Sharaya stood up from where she was sitting and grabbed her boots. She did it slowly, as we were talking, so that I hardly knew it was happening. She brought them back to her seat at the table, and began to put them on. Without much thought, I put down my coffee mug and started putting my shoes on too. She handed me my coat off of the rack and then took her own, and we both zipped them to the top.

"I think if we can get our short lists done in the next three weeks—by January 1st—we can probably move on to the next level. See, that wasn't so bad, was it? Your list is totally doable!"

I caught myself nodding.

"It's just one little baby step at a time," she continued. "If you try to figure out how to do everything, all at once, you'll get overwhelmed. But if you just focus on one task at a time, and keep walking in the same direction, all those little steps add up over time. These things are always more possible than they seem."

It all sounded so nice, but she had to be missing something, didn't she? It couldn't just be this easy—just make a list of four "small" tasks, give ourselves some arbitrary deadline, and then all of a sudden we would be ready to quit our lives to go on a year-long road trip? You can't just do that, can you? If so, why don't more people do it?

We were in the elevator now, dropping six floors to the lobby. The doors parted, and I followed her through the hallway and to the street where, despite the fact I was six inches taller than she is, I had to jog to keep up.

We rode the streetcar and talked about where we would go and how long it would take.

"I think we should go to all fifty states," Sharaya said, and I felt myself nodding again. I don't know how she always did that to me.

We could cover the continental United States in about six months, Sharaya figured, but what about Alaska and Hawaii? Should we go to those first? Or last? How would we get there? I got out my cell phone calculator and estimated the number of miles we would drive, and the average price of gas across the country. We talked about the cost of food and lodging and wondered if, between the two of us, we could find places to stay for free all across the country.

"Fifty states is a lot of states," I told her.

"It was your idea!" she said.

We talked about booking shows and selling merchandise, and Sharaya estimated how much we could make. I compared the two numbers. They were nowhere close. I looked out the window. "This whole thing would be nothing short of a miracle," I said. We both stood holding the handrail on the streetcar, which was slowly rocking our bodies back and forth.

Sharaya looked at me. "I think it's possible," she said.

Not much later we arrived at Powell's, where we wandered up and down the aisles, through the blue room and the rose room, up the stairs to the purple room where the maps were, and I felt it starting to happen. Maybe it was Sharaya. Maybe it was the maps. Maybe this whole crazy thing was contagious. But for whatever reason, this sense of excitement started to bubble up. *What if we made this work?* I wondered to myself. What if we went on a fifty-state road trip?

We wandered down the stairs again to the poetry section. I held two maps in my hand and scanned the rows to see if there were any new collections I needed. I found one I loved and flipped to a familiar page. There it was. The perfect poem. And maybe it was stupid, but mixed with the slight buzz of the coffee and the excitement of the trip, finding that poem in that moment felt important. It felt like some kind of road sign pointing the way to something big and beautiful just up ahead. I read just the first few lines of Billy Collins's *Aristotle* out loud.

"This is the beginning," I said, "almost anything can happen. This is where you find the creation of light, a fish wriggling onto land, the first word of *Paradise Lost* on an empty page . . ." my voice trailed off.

I put the book down carefully, like I might break something if I moved too fast.

"Let's do it," I said to Sharaya, and grinned.

BABY STEPS

Over the next few weeks, Sharaya's words rang in my head: "Don't try to figure out the whole problem; just take small steps, and those things add up over time." I kept that in mind as I called about my school loans, and as I listened to the woman on the other end of the phone tell me I could defer them—five times over the course of the loan, in fact—for any number of reasons, none of which I had to explain in much detail or prove with any sort of hard evidence. Loss of income. Financial hardship. All I had to do was fill out a form. She was polite to me, and I was apologetic, and she told me I didn't need to be. This was her job, after all.

Feeling jazzed from the accomplishment, I called a mechanic friend of mine and told him I would pay him $50 if he would take a look at my car and make sure it was safe to go on a long road trip. He agreed, except for the $50 part. He changed my air filters and my oil, and recommended that I use "high-mileage" oil from now on, but told me that the particular make and model I was driving was reliable and safe. I probably wouldn't have any problem.

This is all too easy, I thought to myself.

I still had to talk to Rebecca, which couldn't possibly be as easy as the other tasks because, no matter how many times I rehearsed the conversation in my head, it never seemed to come out right. "So, I was thinking of quitting my job to travel across the country for six months, leaving you here, alone, to pay the rent all by yourself. But the good news is I'm going to write a book about it! How does that sound?" There was just no good way to spin it. What if she told me that she wanted me to move out for good? Or that I would have to stay until our lease was up? Or that I would have to pay rent while I was gone? I wouldn't be able to afford that.

Finally, one afternoon we went on a run together, and I broached the topic. "I have an idea," I told her. We jogged through the rolling West Hills while we talked, slow and steady, so we could run and talk at the same time. We were seasoned runners. This was normal for us. Something about the distraction and euphoria of running made difficult conversations just a little easier.

I told her everything at once, pausing only to take breaths, but not turning to see her reaction. I told her about where the idea had come from, how Sharaya and I had talked at the wedding, and what we were thinking about doing now. I told her that I never wanted to put her in a difficult position, and that I would do everything I could to find her another roommate if she wanted one, but that I really wanted to live with her when I got back.

We rounded a steep hill, and we both labored for breath. She stopped. I braced myself for the worst.

"I think you're brave," she said, "And I'm sure we can work something out."

Sometimes we make problems so much more difficult than they need to be. I've racked my brain for why we do this, and I can't figure it out. But I wonder if it gives us a good excuse, a way out of doing anything dangerous. I wonder if giving people so little credit for the way they feel about us takes the pressure off of ourselves, and puts it on them. *They* become the reason we're not taking a risk. They couldn't possibly understand, we tell ourselves. Either way, our tendency to dream up conflict before it even exists, to assume we'll encounter all kinds of problems we couldn't possibly predict ahead of time, so often keeps us stranded.

It isn't until we're honest about who we really are, and what we're really feeling, that we give others a chance to show us how brave they think we are. It isn't until we believe in ourselves to do something radical that we invite others to believe with us. And it isn't until those we trust tell us we're trustworthy and brave that we actually realize how trustworthy and brave we really are.

The very best of ideas usually happen this way—all together, in a quiet, messy, community leap.

WHAT'S MISSING?

Sharaya finished her EP and started booking shows in the area. During the day I went to school, where I edited essays and taught kids the correct use of apostrophes and exclamation points, but at night, I would go with Sharaya to her shows. I would follow her around, carry her guitar, and convince her that no one was going to boo her off stage. I liked sitting behind the merchandise table in the back of the room, where it looked like I had a reason to be there but didn't have to talk to anyone. I liked the way I could get free coffee, or soda, or beer when I said "I'm with the band," and how that was like my secret key in the front door. I liked taking video, and tweeting about the event. I liked inviting all the people we knew. I liked laying my notebook open on my lap and writing down thoughts as they came to me during her show. Most of the thoughts died before they saw the light of day, but every once in a while they would become blog posts—and the start of a long tradition to come.

Sharaya offered to let me use her Wordpress account as the blog for our road trip. It already existed, and she had hired someone to design the banner for her, so it looked really professional—more professional than anything I knew how to do. So I agreed and was thankful. We titled the blog "Packing Light."

The idea came from a story in the Gospels of a "rich young ruler." If you've grown up in church, like I have, this passage is familiar. A young man comes to Jesus and gives him his resume. I've done *this* and *that* to be a good man, he says. The more I read the story, the more I identified with him. He wanted to make sure he was doing everything right—making all the right decisions, choosing all the right turns. But after telling Jesus all the great stuff he's done, he asks, "So what else do I have to do to get to heaven?" Jesus answers him, but I'm certain it wasn't the answer he was expecting.

"Sell everything you own and give it to the poor."

Again, growing up in church, I'd heard this story several dozen times. Most of the time, I heard it preached like this: God doesn't want us to be rich. Poor people have an easier time understanding their need for God, so Jesus doesn't want this man to have nice things because his things get in the way of him loving God. Like this young man, we should also avoid having nice things because nice things get in the way of our relationship with Jesus.

I guess, in a way, I can understand that interpretation. There are threads of truth in it. But the problem I always encountered was that I don't think Jesus hates our stuff. In fact, I think Jesus wants us to have a great life, filled with abundance and joy—so much that He was willing to give to hurting people things they didn't actually "need" like food, wine, healing, health.

I also find it interesting that the young ruler came to Jesus in the first place. He was committed to "doing the right thing" and "being a good person" but, at the end of the day, his strategies weren't working. That's what his question to Jesus says to me. It's almost like he's saying, "Okay, I've done all the stuff that You asked me to do, but I still feel dead inside. There has to be something more than this—isn't there? Please tell me there's more. How do I get to *heaven*?" Not "heaven" as in the place you go after you die but heaven as in the Kingdom of Heaven, the taste of heaven that we get to experience every day here on earth.

Jesus says all you have to do is let go, and what you're asking for is at your fingertips. But the young man walks away—because it doesn't make any sense. He already had a pretty good life. He was worried, I'm sure, what would happen if he gave up this life, hoping there might be something better. What if he was worse off than what he had in the first place? Then what?

I felt the same way. I had the job, the apartment, the family, the church, and all the stuff I could ever want, but I was missing something. Wasn't I? I didn't know exactly what it was, but I knew there was something. And I wondered if God was saying to me— just like He was saying to the "rich young ruler"—that if I let go of everything, I would find what I had always wanted. I hoped that was right. I prayed it was right. But honestly, part of me wondered if I would end up worse off than when I started, too.

I would sit down at my computer to record the ideas I was having and would feel this surge of energy, this inexplicable thing creep up inside of me that would distract me from my previously strict schedule. It was so invigorating, in fact, that it kept ruining my nine o'clock bedtime, and my five o'clock wake-up call. It would come over me during my prep period at work, or my lunch hour. I would have an idea and think, *I'm just going to get this on paper really quick,* and before I knew it, a whole hour would pass, and middle school kids would be rushing into my room. It was the strangest sensation, and I wasn't sure where it was coming from, but I liked it. I felt more awake, more alive than ever.

"It's so weird to think about," I told Sharaya as I dropped her off at her apartment one Wednesday, just around midnight. "A month ago I thought ten thirty was a late night." We laughed. But that was only a taste of the changes to come.

SELLING EVERYTHING

You don't realize how much junk you have until you try to put it all in a box. It sounds stupid, but it's true. I am not a pack rat—in fact just the opposite. I move fairly often, and each time I get rid of things that seem unimportant. But this time, as I went through my house and loaded everything I owned into boxes to be sold at our yard sale, I couldn't believe how much stuff there was. Clothes. Yoga mats. Crockpots. CDs. Electronics. Golf clubs. Furniture. Books. What's more, I couldn't believe how much I liked all of it.

"Are we really doing this?" I asked Sharaya nervously as we loaded the first batch of things into the back of a friend's borrowed truck.

"Yeah, why?" she asked coyly. "Are you having second thoughts?"

I wasn't sure. But if I was, there was no time to stop and wonder.

We opened a joint bank account so that we could keep track of all the expenses for the trip. We started plotting our journey and booking shows. We transported all of our things to my parents' garage, little by little, where they had agreed to let us host our sale. We made personal investments to the bank account, and created a video for Kickstarter to crowd source the funds required to get up and go. We announced our trip to our family members and our Bible study, and held our breath while we waited to hear their reactions. We promised anyone who donated $100 to our cause that we would collect fifty postcards for them, one from each of the fifty states (which I realized meant we actually had to go to them). These weren't baby steps anymore. This was real commitment. I felt it creep up and overwhelm me with heaviness, my last chance to pull the release valve before I couldn't back out anymore.

Then, one Saturday, I told Sharaya I didn't want to go.

We were sitting at Sip & Kranz, a coffee shop in the Pearl District of Portland just blocks from her apartment, dwarfed by the giant chairs and the fear of what we both felt was coming. There were maps in front of us, all spread out and promising, bigger than the table that we had even set them on. I think she knew I was about to say something awful. She had that look on her face. Her head was cocked and she was waiting.

"I can't do it," I said.

I wished it were all a joke. I wished that I could just laugh and tell her that I was kidding, that I wasn't having second thoughts about everything. But instead all I could think about was how, if I left Portland now, I would ruin everything. I would never figure out what I was supposed to do with my life. I would never just settle down and be normal. I would never get married. After all, I was twenty-six years old. If I didn't settle down now, when would I?

"You can decide not to go on this trip," she told me. "But I promise you'll regret it."

I hung my head.

I went home early that night and thought about what she said. Would I regret it? So much could happen in the course of six months. I would miss so much. Going would mean I would have to give up my job, my apartment, my stuff, my friends, my life. Sure, going on this trip *could* mean getting the life I always wanted. It could mean that I would get to write a book. But what if it didn't? What if I lost everything in the process? What if going on this trip meant that I would never get a life like I wanted? What if the only way to get the kind of life I wanted was to stay put?

I went to bed at eight-forty-five because I was sick of being tired all the time. I was sick of traipsing around with Sharaya to all her shows just to sit in the back of the room and take pictures. I was sick of giving up sleep for some stupid road trip. What was the point, anyway? A road trip wasn't going to change my life, was it? As I drifted off, the doubts ran like some some stupid slide show on the backs of my eyelids. *If I didn't go, I would regret it.* I wanted to punch those words in the face and tell them to go you-know-where.

While I slept, I dreamed I was in Costa Rica. I had traveled there the previous summer so the setting was familiar to me. In fact, the images playing in my mind were burned in my memory— so realistic it seemed hard to distinguish between dream and reality.

In my dream, I stood on the edge of a waterfall—about thirty-five feet high. I watched several people hurl themselves over the edge, pierce the water with alarming force, and emerge again, smiling. I wanted to do it, but I was afraid.

It happened in my dream the same way it happened in real life the previous summer. I handed my camera to a bystander and instructed him to take video. Gingerly, I found my way to a rock that jetted out above the falls. I widened my stance, put my right foot securely in front of my left, and leaned out over the edge of the water. From there, I stared at my inevitable path down.

In real life, when you watch that video, you can hear the boy taking the video scream to me, "Do it, do it!" You can hear me scream back, "I don't want to die. I just don't want to die." Then, seconds later, you watch my legs rock back and forth, and finally spring me over the edge. You see me career down to the bottom of the falls. A crowd of bystanders cheers me on and the video keeps running until my head pops out of the water. I'm beaming, so proud of my accomplishment.

In my dream, however, when the boy yelled, "Do it, do it!" I said nothing. I peered out over the edge, looked at the fall, shook my head, and turned to walk away. That's where the dream ended.

I woke up thinking about the "rich young ruler." He came to Jesus, just like I did to the waterfall. Nobody forced him to come. He came voluntarily. Maybe, like me, he saw others take the leap before him and experience something thrilling. Maybe, like me, he was drawn by the beauty of the waterfall itself. Either way, he came without force. He widened his stance, put one foot in front of the other, braced himself, and then paused to ask the question: *How do I get a taste of heaven?*

Jesus gave him an answer. Jump, He said. Do it! "Sell everything you own, and give it to the poor," Jesus told him. "Then come follow Me." The young man looked at Jesus, much the same that

I must have looked at that waterfall in my dream, and decided it wasn't worth it. Too dangerous. Too much of a risk.

Sometimes I wonder if the story of the rich young ruler is more about fear than anything. That's what I thought about as I lay in bed that morning.

Everyone is afraid to lose something—dignity, reputation, comfort, safety, stuff. It's easy to look at someone who has something you don't and wonder, "You're not willing to give up *that*? What's the big deal?" It's easy for me to look at the "rich young ruler" and think how sad it is he wouldn't give up his "riches" in order to follow Jesus. That's because I'm not very rich (at least not compared to the people living right around me). But all of us have "riches" we don't want to sacrifice to follow Jesus. For some of us it's comfort, for others it's image, and for others still it's relationships. Yes, even relationships can get in the way of heaven.

What if the things we feel most attached to are the things standing between us and heaven? Not "heaven" as in the place we go when we die, but heaven as in the tangible perception of God's peace, love, and mercy, breaking into our reality and our lives right now. We taste it in a delicious meal, a glass of wine, a first kiss, or a conversation with friends. We taste it when we laugh until we hurt, and when we love something so much we're willing to give up whatever it takes to get it.

What if these "things" we're attached to aren't even bad things, but our fear of losing them is keeping us from seeing *beyond* what we have right now? What if there is something better?

What am I so afraid to lose? I wondered as I stared at my spinning ceiling fan. I had spent so much of my life putting off what I really wanted because I was worried about the future. I had saved instead of spent, eaten vegetables instead of cheeseburgers, studied instead of played. I had spent so much energy fighting against my desires, making the decision that may not have felt good now, but that was best for later. I was trying to be wise. But what if my desires were telling me something? What if the decision that was good for now was also good for later? What if I just couldn't see it yet?

I felt the realization settle over me, like the weight of my comforter against my tired body. Unless I let go of what I was holding, I would never get the answers to my deepest questions: Is God good? Can I trust Him? Will He provide for me? Should I jump into the waterfall?

So I woke up and called Sharaya and told her I was sorry, that I didn't know what had gotten into me but that she could count on me. I was all in. Then I hung up the phone and bartered with God.

"Okay, I'll go," I told Him. "But please don't make me be alone forever."

The next day I met Benjamin.

3

say goodbye

"Life is about the not knowing, the delicious and often terrifying ambiguity, having to change, accommodate...taking the moment and making the the best of it, without knowing what is next."

GILDA RADNER

IT WAS LATE AFTERNOON and I was walking into a coffee shop in northwest Portland when he spotted me. "Ally?" he said out loud, and it wasn't until he looked at me that I remembered what I was wearing: a long, blue summer dress that hugged my figure, simple but elegant. I turned to see his face. Something about the way he was looking at me—a combination of joy and awe—suddenly made me feel very pretty. And I felt a rush of that certain sense of consciousness that comes with being noticed.

Recognition came over me like a slow wave. I knew that face. I recognized his height, which was enough that I had to lift my chin to see him, then the boldness of his stature, then the shape of his jaw, the specific way his eyes wrinkled as a broad smile spread across his face. His features took me, for just a split second, back to the internship I had worked the summer before I left for college. Was it really eight years ago? And it was that momentary journey that tumbled me into the full wave of memory.

"Ben," I said out loud, once I reoriented myself to where we were, in real time, and to the reality of this unexpected meeting. We both stood there for a minute, looking at each other, with some combination of intrigue and attraction. I think we both felt that if one of us broke the silence, the feeling would go away. So we held on for as long as we could.

He spoke first, and asked me what I was doing these days. I only half-listened, focusing more on keeping my hands from shaking and my voice from shaking than on the words coming out of his mouth. I told him I would tell him about my life, but first he had to tell me about his. It was the only way I could think to buy myself time to catch my breath and at the same time keep our conversation from ending prematurely.

He talked about getting his master's degree, about traveling all over the world, and about the company he was working for now, where he was really happy. We briefly talked about a few of our mutual friends.

"Okay, now it's your turn!" he said, and I giggled a little.

"How much time do you have?"

"I've got all day," he said.

LOVE AND TACOS

I'm not sure whose idea it was to go to dinner together that night, but looking back, I would like to say it was his. He had made it pretty clear he was interested in hearing about me and my life since we'd last met, and I wanted to tell him about the road trip. So we walked the neighborhoods of northwest Portland, the perfect time of year to be outside and walking. Temperatures were rising, blossoms were forming, and you could almost smell the imminence of spring. The trees reached their sweet arms over the top of our heads as we walked, and I secretly wondered what it would be like to have Ben reach his arm around my shoulders. We passed several open doors before settling on a small Mexican restaurant. We ordered tacos and I started from the beginning.

I told him that I had always loved to write, and that I was actually pretty good at it. He smiled, and told me he already knew that. I blushed. It had been so long since I felt this—this body and soul sensation of being seen, and enjoyed.

We sat at a little table for two in the back corner of a hole-in-the-wall taco joint, but it might as well have been the most romantic place in the city. The gentle way he looked at me, the quiet and peaceful way he listened. I was overcome.

I shared how my love for writing had driven me to get a bachelor's degree in English, and how I felt like the obvious venue for using my strengths was teaching, so I had gotten my master's in teaching. I talked about how hard it all was, but how the affirmation I received for my job seemed to keep me going, and how I figured everything would work itself out around graduation.

He nodded, like he understood.

I told Ben about substitute teaching for a full year before finally landing a full-time job as a middle school teacher.

"It felt like such an accomplishment at the time," I told him. "The economy was tough, and there weren't that many jobs for teachers. I was so excited to finally get started with my career."

"I can relate," he said, gesturing for me to help myself to our chips and salsa.

Then I told him about that sinking feeling I would get each morning as I drove to school. *Something's missing*, I would think to myself, but I would try to talk myself out of it. *Everyone must feel this way,* I reasoned. After all, I was lucky to have this job. Some people didn't have that luxury. So many of the students who had graduated with me were still substitute teaching. I would chastise myself for not being more grateful, and encourage myself to get a grip.

I continued. *You can do this, you can do this, you can do this,* I would tell myself over and over again, on the drive to work, and on the drive home. And each day, at the end of the day, I would find out that I was right. I did do it. I made it through a day, and then a month, and then a semester, and then a full school year. It wasn't that the job was hard, although it was. It was that time was just sort of passing.

Ben listened intently, asked good questions, and I loved that. He even leaned in over the table while he listened to me, like he didn't want to miss a thing.

It wasn't until I started talking to Sharaya, I told him, that I really started to feel it, this thing I couldn't really explain. It's like an energy, a resolve, an overwhelming sensation that this is the best of me. I told him about sitting down to write, and how time would just fly by. I told him about the idea of writing a book, and how, for the first time in as long as I could remember, I really wanted something. I used my hands while I talked, and couldn't stop smiling, and seemed to have forgotten completely about my tacos.

"Each day I woke up and felt like I was chasing after something, something that really mattered to me. Sharaya gave me permission to admit I wanted something better. Does that make sense?" He nodded gently.

"Do you think I'm crazy?"

"Yes," he smiled. "And I love it. So what now?" he asked.

I told him about how the idea was born. I told him everything—about the wedding, about waffling back and forth for so long, about calling about the school loans, and telling Rebecca, and how we were going to sell everything to raise money. I told him about how I had found myself, more recently, staying up late at Sharaya's shows, or writing blog posts, and about the excitement that bubbled up in me every time we would lay a map in front of us to chart our course.

"Teacher by day, vagabond by night," he joked, and I laughed.

Then the two of us just sat in silence for a minute, dodging eye contact but at the same time desperate to look at the other, desperate to know what the other was thinking.

"It's the weirdest thing," I said finally. "I'm busier now than I've ever been. I'm more tired. My life is a total wreck. But I'm happier too. Is that crazy?"

He shook his head, and I took a bite of my taco.

"Have you ever felt bored with your life?" I asked.

"Of course," he said and paused for a minute. "Then I lost my job and I had to ask myself some of the same questions you're asking. I had to re-prioritize and re-organize. Sometimes it takes losing everything to find out what is really important." He looked down at his plate when he said the words "lost my job," flicking his gaze down and back up. I locked eyes with him as if to say—it's okay.

I told him about this book I read a few months ago called *A Million Miles in a Thousand Years* by Donald Miller, and how he said all good stories have a character who *wants* something and is willing to give up whatever it takes to get it. It occurred to me while I was reading the book, I told him, that I was going through my whole life without really wanting anything. The things I wanted I figured were out of my reach, and so I spent most of my time reaching for things I was "supposed" to have. A successful career. A paycheck. A nice home. A nine-to-five.

I woke up every day and went through the motions, but I felt lifeless. A passionless life was a safe life, but it was a boring life. It was scary to want something, I told him. Wanting something meant feeling the pain of not having it, and feeling the pain of chasing it down. I played with the straw in my glass, scared to look across the table, scared to know if he was looking at me.

"I think we have to let go of some stuff in order to get what we really want."

"You're inspiring," he said.

What I didn't tell him was that I had almost backed out of the trip altogether. I didn't tell him because I didn't want him to stop looking at me the way he was, full of awe and admiration. In every other way I abandoned myself to our conversation, sharing from the deepest part of myself, praying he would accept it for what it was, but I held that small part back. It didn't occur to me that, if I told him, he may have understood. After all, we're all scared of wanting something, scared of taking risks, of living outside of "normal." Just like the "rich young ruler," we're all afraid to give up what we have because we're worried we'll never have anything better.

He asked me questions, but I didn't feel like I was being quizzed. I responded and, as I did, I felt important—like there was nowhere else in the world he wanted to be except right there, listening to me, looking at me. We ate and talked, and I melted into a space where two hours feels like three days, and three days feels like five minutes, and five minutes feels like a lifetime.

"If you had to pitch your trip in one sentence, what would it be?" Ben asked.

It was a good question—I thought for a few minutes before answering.

"I think it would just be that we're experimenting. We're experimenting living a life where nothing holds us back. Not what we expected out of life, or what other people expected out of us, not fear or insecurity, not the stuff that we accumulate in our house. We're packing light. We don't promise we're good at it, but we're trying it. And then I plan to write about it." I laughed, because it all sounded so wonderful and ridiculous. I was sure this was the best idea I had ever had in my life, but it was also the craziest. And putting it into words like that made me reckless because it made it real.

He walked me to my car, and for the first time I became conscious of it—the thing I had wanted for so long, but could never seem to summon, or that was unpredictable and fleeting. I tried to talk myself out of it, reasoning that the timing was terrible, and thinking of how badly it would hurt to find he didn't feel what I was feeling. But talking yourself out of falling in love is like talking yourself out of being bronzed by rays of the sun. And when Ben asked me for my number, I couldn't resist.

"Only if I can have yours," I said, and smiled.

After that night, my busy schedule suddenly started to seem very open. All the things on my "to-do" list that had once seemed important began to fade into the background. Hosting a yard sale, selling our things, packing for the trip, saying goodbye to friends, finishing the school year—all these things were background noise to what was unfolding in front of me. Not that they weren't important, but I floated through them—happier than I had been in a long time. Ben and I went on walks and to dinner parties and stayed up too late talking. He came with me to Sharaya's shows. I would get dressed up to meet him, and he would look at me and shake his head, without saying anything. Sometimes he would leave the city for a few days, on business, and send me a postcard. He called it "practicing." Then one Saturday, a week before I left for six months, we talked over grilled salmon and glasses of red wine about life and faith and what we were thinking.

"I bought a Bible," he told me.

I looked up from my plate. I wasn't expecting him to say that.

"I've been a Christian my whole life," he continued, "but I've never seen anyone live it out like you're doing. I listen to you talk about your life and I want what you have. I know what you're doing must be really scary, but it's changing people, Ally. It's really important."

I listened while he told me about how he had started reading in Genesis, and was going to read through all the way to the end. He told me he had found an old book by C. S. Lewis on his bookshelf, and he was going to start reading that too. His face lit up as we talked, and I knew something important was happening between us. I knew Ben would be a part of my story, and that I would be a part of his too.

"Since I met you . . ." His voice trailed off. "I just see it." His lip quivered a bit as he said it. I put my fork down and reached my hand across the table.

"Do you know I don't think it's an accident we reconnected?"

"I know you're leaving," he told me. "But I can't pretend like this didn't happen."

I know you aren't supposed to barter with God. That's not how it works. That's not how any relationship works.

But in this case, I'll be honest, I felt like it *had* worked like that. The morning I woke up from my waterfall dream I told God I would give up everything. I also told Him exactly what I wanted in return. Then with one wild and resolute push, I flung myself over the edge. Now, here was Ben. He was sitting right in front of me. Was it the result of a barter? Or, was it an act of obedience and a demonstration of love in return? I didn't really know. All I could think was: *He cared for me.* Ben did, and God did.

"I'm not asking you to wait for me," I said.

"You don't have to. I'm offering."

So that night I drove home with what felt like the most valuable gift I had ever been given—as beautiful as it was fragile. And although it was a new gift to me, I could barely imagine what life was like without it. I took a deep breath.

I prayed God would show me where to put this gift He had given, how to care for it, and how to keep it from shattering in my grip.

4

embrace the unexpected

"I know what it is to be in need, and I know what it is to have plenty.
I have learned the secret of being content in any and every situation,
whether well fed or hungry, whether living in plenty or in want."
APOSTLE PAUL (PHILIPPIANS 4:12)

PACKING THE CAR WAS an art. Everything had a place, and a reason it was in that place. We had a finely tuned system.

The sound equipment, merchandise, and Sharaya's guitar were in the trunk, so that you couldn't see them when we parked on the street. Those were the things most likely to be stolen, we figured, so it was best to hide them where no one could see them. As for the rest of the stuff, there was no getting around leaving some of it in the back of the car, but we would try to be strategic about it. We parked our suitcases behind each of our seats respectively, and hung a clothing rack between the two back windows, so our favorite dresses and shirts didn't get too wrinkled or dirty.

Below the clothes was a cooler filled with snacks and bottles of water, where we could access it easily if we got hungry or thirsty on the road. We borrowed a cargo box for the top of the car, the kind that attaches to your ski rack, and kept any extras (shampoo, hair products, deodorant, razors, etc.) we thought we might need there. We could have purchased these things along the way, but since they were already sitting under our sinks when we cleaned out our apartments, and we weren't exactly sure how much money we were going to make, we brought them with us.

Everything was intentional. Everything had purpose. Each piece was nestled against the other like a jigsaw puzzle.

That doesn't mean we brought everything we wanted to. In fact, as we packed the car two days before we left the city, it looked a little like we were having a second yard sale outside my apartment. The car was parked between several open spots, and all around it the pavement was covered with boxes of shoes and bags full of coats that we weren't sure we would need, and enough books to last through all fifty states. For all our intentions of packing light, it still seemed like stuff was everywhere.

But when it doesn't all fit, you make value judgements. Do you really need twenty books, or can you live with just ten? Do you need four coats, or will two be okay? Can we share clothes and bring less of them? Can we get rid of this extra shampoo and just buy the cheap stuff while we're on the road? There wasn't room for all of our shoes. It was either the books or the shoes—which do you pick?

When everything doesn't fit, you have to get rid of some of it. You stand there, for hours maybe, making decisions that feel sort of painful because you just don't have quite enough information. You're not sure how to prepare, and what unexpected bends in the road will arise, and what you might need when they do. And what you land on in the end feels very final—like you've gotten down to the bare minimum.

This is what it felt like during the few days before our trip—like we were getting down to the bare minimum.

The night before we left, I made the rounds to say my good-byes. I started with family—an evening filled with hugs, grilled chicken on the porch, road safety reminders, and promises to call at least once a week. Then I went to hang out with Rebecca, in our apartment that was suddenly and strangely devoid of all my things. But the one person I wanted to see most was out of town.

He was on a business trip. He wouldn't be back until early the next morning, about the same time we'd be hitting the road. The timing was awful, but at the same time this was going to be the reality of our relationship for the next six months at least. We'd better get used to it.

The morning of our departure Sharaya and I carried the last few things down—purses, computers, makeup bags, that sort of thing—from Rebecca's apartment. We climbed into the car and drove toward the freeway, without too much dialogue. Sharaya drove toward I-5 North, and just as we were passing through downtown, she took a familiar exit. I was pretty sure I knew what she was doing.

She took a right and a left, and the closer we got the more sure I became. Left on Glisan, right on 20th, all the way to Savier. Without a word, she pulled up to her surprise location—Ben's house.

"Take your time," she said.

I ran up two flights of stairs and knocked on his door.

"Surprise!" I smiled.

He scooped me up and swung me around so the last bit of cof-fee in his cup nearly splashed out onto the back of my shirt. For the next several minutes there were no words exchanged, just arms tangled and looks shared and little pinprick tears threatening to make a break for it and run down my face.

"I have to go," I said finally.

"I'm not ready," he whispered back, but he still let me go.

I walked back down the stairs, much more slowly than I had come up, and turned to take one last look at him standing in the doorway before climbing back into the car.

"Ready?" Sharaya asked.

"Ready or not," I replied.

And with that, we were on our way.

RULES OF THE ROAD

"We need to come up with a list of rules," Sharaya said, once we were speeding down the highway.

She was in the driver's seat, and I was secure on the passenger side.

"Rules for what?" I asked.

"For the trip," she said. "You know, so we're still friends at the end of this."

I laughed and reached for my notebook, which was tucked away in my purse, sitting conveniently at my feet. "I'll write them down," I told Sharaya.

"Maybe you could even turn it into a blog post," she said.

"All right, you start," I told her, since it hadn't occurred to me to come up with rules before she suggested it.

"No clicking pens," she said, without much hesitation.

I laughed. "Really?" From the look on her face I gathered that she was not kidding.

"Okay, I can do that," I told her. "What else?"

"I think we should have a rule for listening to music," she said. "I thought that we could take turns listening to an entire album of our choice, but the person who didn't choose the album isn't allowed to complain to the person who did choose it."

"That sounds fair," I said.

"Perfect, write it down," she said, and I did.

We came up with other rules too, more serious ones. We decided that we were going to pray together every time we left a city and that, each day, we would affirm each other in three ways. It might sound cheesy or overkill, but we knew what could happen when you put friendship in stressful situations. Sharaya wanted to play music and I wanted to write a book, but we knew none of our personal goals would be very rewarding if we weren't having fun together.

We promised to check the oil at least once a week, and before every long drive, and that we would try to come to an agreement about everything before we made final decisions. We promised to be open with each other, and honest about what we were feeling. It all sounded pretty simple. After all, this wasn't rocket science—it was just friendship.

The rules would keep us safe, we thought, like a fence on a playground. They would draw a line around us and make sure no harm could get inside. They would make sure no oblivious child ran after a stray ball right in front of a speeding semi.

We continued up I-5 North to Seattle, and I texted with Ben periodically. He told me he missed me already, and the truth was I missed him too. I knew this was part of it, part of the journey, and that one day we would be grateful. I pictured us telling this story to our kids, or our grandkids. It would seem so romantic later, even though right now it felt excruciating.

We passed Centralia, then Tacoma, then Kent and Federal Way, and I tried to draw myself into the moment. Yes, I missed Ben, but moping about missing him wouldn't make the next six months go by any faster. In fact, it would probably make them miserable. I didn't want to miss this. So I put my phone away, picked up my head, and looked resolutely out the window. *Here we go,* I told myself. Before we knew it, we saw the city of Seattle rise up from the horizon. We celebrated our arrival, the first small step in our long journey.

JUST LIKE HOME

Sharaya's first show in Seattle was at a pizza parlor, and we headed directly there. The whole thing felt so normal. We had just commenced on the most radical journey of our lives, yet there was something really familiar about it too. We didn't have to think about it, it was just there—like running into an old friend. You just know that you know this person, and that they are safe. It was the same way with Seattle—the way the buildings looked, the way the people dressed, the notion that, if we left now, we could probably be back in Portland by dinner.

Then there was the pizza place itself, which could just as easily have been set in Portland. The booths were deep red, and the floors were checkered black and white. Everything was a little dingy inside because that's how hipsters like it. There was a painting of Elvis on one wall, with yarn glued to the canvas as his hair, and a modge-podge of objects tacked to the ceiling, from Barbies to bike wheels. It would have been easy to write the place off as strange or dirty, but to us it felt homey.

Checking in with the owner felt almost like an old habit, since we had rehearsed it so many times before. "I'm scheduled to play here tonight," Sharaya would say as she introduced herself. "Oh, yes," the owner would respond with recognition, and kindly show us where to go. Sharaya looked at the setup for sound and then we would unload. "Hold this," she would say, or "Take this inside." I didn't have to know anything about sound or music, I just had to follow her lead. We had a comfortable rhythm—a flow.

It was the first of a hundred times we would do this on the road—unload the car according to our system and set up our different stations inside. Sharaya would run the sound check, and I would set up the merchandise table. She would do her voice warm-ups, and I would tweet about the event. She would worry no one was going to come, and if they did, that they might hate her. I would assure her that was impossible.

Sharaya was the most fearless person I had ever met, except for the last hour before she took the stage. I guess everyone is afraid of something.

As for me, while she was on stage wowing the audience with her talent, I sat back and enjoyed the show. I liked my place by the merchandise table. It was safe and comfortable. I didn't need a stage. I didn't need the stress. This was my element. Friends and strangers came that night, as they did many nights over the course of our trip. I talked to them some, but I also kept to myself in moments, thinking thoughts and writing them in my notebook.

When Sharaya was on stage with her guitar, and I was at the back table with my pen, we were both exactly where we belonged.

My friend Dana from college came with her two friends. They all commented on Sharaya's beautiful voice. An old friend from church had recently moved to Seattle and seen the update I posted on Facebook. He brought his wife to the show. Another friend was in town on a business trip. I migrated back and forth between my cluster of friends on one side of the restaurant and my private space, by the merchandise table, on the other. We ate pizza and chicken Caesar salad for dinner, part of Sharaya's payment for performing. *This was so simple,* I thought to myself. It hardly even felt like we left home.

AN UNEXPECTED INVITATION

It was a last-minute decision to ride the ferry to Bainbridge Island. Neither of us had ever been before, and our friend Travis offered to buy our tickets. He wasn't a close friend, but we learned as early as Seattle that when you're far from home, you never turn up your nose to friendship or free tickets to anything. Each time we would arrive in a new place we would try to find someone we knew, and someone who knew our new location, so they could introduce us. Travis was that person.

So the three of us found cheap parking—fifteen blocks up a hill from the boarding dock—and huffed and puffed our way to the entrance. I commented about how Seattle was a good butt workout, and Sharaya said I should tweet that, so I did.

We handed our tickets to the attendant and, as we stepped on the boat, I felt a gust of wind pull my long dark hair off the back of my neck. We stood along the rails, cell phones and sunglasses tightly secured as we leaned over and felt the boat pull away from land. This is what road trips and adventures were supposed to feel like—wild and carefree. It was a perfect Pacific Northwest summer day.

We found a market on the island where we bought bread, cheese, and hummus, and sat at a picnic table under a tree. We hadn't thought about it, but this would be the first of many meals we would enjoy in a park, with plastic silverware and no plates. Today we lingered even longer than we needed to because, at this point, it was more about the whimsy of it than the necessity. Though later down the road, there would be moments we would do anything for the "luxury" of eating with real silverware at a real table.

We played Frisbee and talked about what we would be doing if we were home right now. "I'd probably be working at a restaurant," I said, "you know, since teachers get paid so much." Sharaya remarked how she would probably be showing a house this morning, or finishing up paperwork in the office.

"Must be nice to be living the high life!" Travis joked.

We laughed and talked and lingered—letting the satisfaction of lunch and the heat of the afternoon sink in. We lost track of time until Sharaya's phone buzzed with an email.

The senders of the email, Sean and Eva, weren't sure exactly how they had found our website, but were intrigued by what we were doing. "What *are* you doing, by the way?" they added. They wanted to know more about our adventure, and they knew it was weird, given that we had never met them, but they wanted to know if we would be willing to come over to share our story sometime. They would make dinner for us. They left their number and told us to call if we were interested.

Sharaya and I looked at each other, exchanging silent messages. Should we call the number? Should we just ignore it? I mean, it was just a phone call, wasn't it? Of course there was risk involved, but wasn't that what this trip was all about—taking risks? Isn't that why we were here—to live good stories? The conversation with my parents kept playing over and over again. "I promise I'll be safe," I had told them.

I kept hearing Ben say, in the back of my mind, "I don't know what I would do if something happened to you."

Travis broke the silence. "I think you girls are over thinking this," he said, "The whole point of a road trip like this is that your life looks different than it did at home. Embrace the unexpected, even if you're not sure how it will turn out."

"Embrace the unexpected!" Sharaya said suddenly.

"Embrace the unexpected!" I echoed, although the words came out of my mouth before I was sure if I meant it.

So as we walked to board the ferry back to the city, I listened to one side of a phone conversation between Eva and Sharaya. "We love Thai food," I heard her say, and, "Tonight sounds perfect. . . . Seven o'clock? Sure, we'll be there."

Just like that—we had our first plan for dinner with strangers.

We didn't know it then, but "embrace the unexpected" would become a common refrain we would use over and over again to guide our journey. Our understanding of what it was—and what it wasn't—was so elementary that I look back now and laugh at the innocence of it all. But perhaps that's part of the beauty. We were doing the best we could with the information we had, the best we knew how with what we had been given. That's all you can expect from anyone. That's all we can ask of ourselves.

We would repeat it at crucial times when we didn't know how else to explain what was going on, as a way to keep ourselves going in the midst of that confusion. We would remind each other when our lodging fell through in Maine, or worse, in New York City (where you really don't want to be sleeping in your car). It would come to mind, inconveniently, during an infamous day in Laramie, Wyoming. When tragedy struck at home, we would whisper it to ourselves quietly: "Embrace the unexpected." We would say it each time—and there were many times—we had to do something that wasn't comfortable.

Sometimes it would be exhilarating, sometimes it would be terrifying, and sometimes perfectly peaceful, like the Frisbee and picnic lunch on Bainbridge Island that day, or like dinner with Sean and Eva.

WHAT DO YOU NEED?

The dinner with Sean and Eva started off as any event with perfect strangers might: awkwardly. But once Eva had offered us drinks and we were all planted comfortably on the living room couches, the conversation started flowing. It wasn't long before we felt like old friends.

"So let me get this straight," Sean said. "You girls just decided that you didn't want full-time jobs anymore, so you quit to go on this road trip?"

He laughed. We were grinning.

"Yeah," I said. "Pretty much."

We tried to explain from the beginning. We talked about how discouraged we were feeling before our trip—like we were living someone else's expectations for our lives instead of doing what we were made to do. We talked about the restlessness we felt, and about realizing the only reason we hadn't pursued the dreams we had for our lives was because, somewhere along the way, we picked up the lie that it wasn't possible for them to happen. We felt like we were letting stuff get in the way.

"I felt like my life was just sort of happening to me," I explained. "Like I was just sitting back and watching it pass by. I wanted to do something, anything, whatever it took to start living again, and stop spectating."

"It's like a jump start," Sharaya said.

We shared openly, and Sean and Eva listened intently. We waited for them to respond with the enthusiasm we felt. Instead, Sean asked, "Are you Christians?"

"Yes," we said.

"Are you going to be a Christian artist?" He looked to Sharaya. She fumbled over her words, trying to explain how she was a musician and a Christian, but not necessarily a Christian musician. But Sean seemed unconvinced. "Looking at your website, I just felt confused. I thought, you're going to have to make it really clear to people. Are you Christian or are you not?"

Are you Christian or are you not? That question stuck with me for weeks, even months, after he had asked it. It was an important question—a helpful one—even though it didn't feel like it at the time. At the time it felt like an attack, like a headlock I wanted to wriggle my way out of. Why did we always have to pick a side? I was a Christian, and I wanted to be a writer, but was I a "Christian writer"? I didn't know.

Did that mean I could only cover certain subjects, or that I had to talk about things in a certain way? Did it mean I had to say certain things about politics and alcohol and how I should date or not date? I loved God, but I didn't love the way people always tried to box God in. I didn't want to be boxed in. I felt my cheeks get warm because I knew the question was going to be asked of me next, and I didn't know what to say.

Eva broke the silence first. "What do you guys need?" she asked, standing up to clear dessert plates.

"Nothing," Sharaya said, putting her hand on her stomach.

"I'm perfectly content," I agreed.

"I don't just mean now," Eva said. "I mean in general. What do you need? For the next six months of travel? What can we do for you? How can we help you?"

I thought about it, but I couldn't come up with anything. Sharaya mentioned something about referrals for venues where we could book shows, and Sean said he knew a guy in Utah—Peter something—who he would connect us with. But me? I couldn't think of anything.

In fact, I pictured our car parked out on the street, filled to the brim with everything from clothes to food to windshield wiper fluid, and I wondered what we would run out of in the next six months. I pondered what we would wish we had two weeks from now, or two months from now, or by the time we rounded the corner toward home.

It occurred to me that this is part of the difficulty of packing light. You have to plan for something you can't possibly understand yet. You have to know what cold feels like before you understand your need for a jacket. If you've never felt hungry, you don't understand your need for food. A person who knows nothing about London wouldn't consider that rain boots might be helpful, and a traveler who has never been to Costa Rica in the winter wouldn't know that, wherever you're going in the city, you should take an umbrella with you in the afternoon. You have to feel a need before you can know it—and plan accordingly.

As for us, we hadn't felt many needs yet. We hadn't allowed ourselves to. We'd provided everything we needed for ourselves, and then some. We hadn't felt hungry, wet, cold, tired, or panicked—yet. That would come later. So right then, we didn't know what we needed. This is the irony with needs. We all have them, but we generally don't discover them until we go without for a while.

We discover what we need when we live without things. This is part of the value of traveling and packing light as we travel. Sometimes it's good for us to need things and not have them.

Other times it's good to have people like Sean and Eva who know what it feels like to need something, and who are willing to meet our need. To me, that's the most tangible picture of compassion and grace—people sharing resources, even when they don't know us, even if they're not totally sure what our journey is about. It's not an obligation. It comes without expectations. We have a need, and they give out of their abundance.

The more I think back about Sean and Eva, and the more I let my memory pass over all the places we visited, I can't help but think: If we weren't willing to let go of things we needed, we never would have gone on a trip. But if people weren't willing to see our need and meet it, we never would have made it back home.

CONSTANTS AND VARIABLES

We had to stay in Seattle for several nights due to the fact that Sharaya had booked three shows over the course of five days. The first two nights we slept at a condo in Everett, just north of the city. Our friends were camping and offered to let us use their place. In the morning we would wake up, make coffee, and walk right out to the Sound where I would jog along the coast and Sharaya would do calisthenics on the sand. We would marvel at our resourcefulness and at the hazy, beautiful view.

During those first few days we tried to come up with a system for what we would bring in and what we would leave in the car each night, but the conclusion wasn't as easy to reach as we thought. We'd bring our small suitcases into the house, and our purses, and everything else would stay. That was our first conclusion, and we were proud of it. But what about the cooler? Would the food last in the car overnight? And what about all the hanging clothes and the extra bag of shoes? If we never brought any of these things in, would we ever wear them? What was a good way to rotate these items? If we kept our makeup bags in our suitcases, how would we get to them during the day, or before a show? These were all discussions that started early on and would last through many states.

The more stuff you bring with you, the more complicated everything gets. Have you ever noticed that? If you pack twelve shirts and four pairs of pants, you'll have forty-eight combinations. That's forty-eight options for what to wear each day! Those options seemed appealing to me while I was packing, but once I was living out of a suitcase, I resented all the choices. Options make decisions really hard and really messy. We had so much stuff, and we were moving all the time. It made it hard to have a system and keep it.

Also, the more stuff you have, the more difficult it is to find anything. Of the twelve shirts you decided to bring, half of them end up buried so deep in your suitcase you forget you even brought them. Your suitcase is heavier than it needs to be, and the one shirt you want you can't find because there is so much extra stuff.

Despite the logistics of our luggage, we tried to maintain some semblance of routine. There was always work to be done. We drove into the city during the day, found a coffee shop where people seemed to be working on their computers (which is not difficult in a city like Seattle, by the way), and would work on booking, promoting, writing press releases, and researching new places to play shows. When all of that was done, I would write a blog post or two. We discussed the fact that I was spending most of my time helping Sharaya with her shows, rather than working on my book, but agreed her music was our only source of income.

"Without your shows, we both go home," I told her.

Finding time to talk to Ben wasn't easy. His hours were pretty consistent, and ours were not. When he was finished with work and free to talk, I would be having dinner with friends, or guarding the merchandise table at Sharaya's show. I started to see how complicated our long-distance relationship was going to be. Still, we did the best we could. We texted each other and stayed up late into the night to write long notes or just catch a few quiet minutes together on the phone. We exchanged funny and embarrassing moments, as well as deep philosophical conversations. I told him how Sharaya noticed I don't screw lids on very tight, and asked him how he was going to feel about this long term. He shared what he was thinking as he read through the book of Genesis.

Ben was always amused by our stories on the road, and we had plenty.

Sharaya and I were creative with our food choices, trying to maximize our finances and leverage opportunities to eat for free. We would buy avocados, cut them in half, and dig into them with tortilla chips. We purchased a huge bag of quinoa from Costco and would cook it in batches, storing it in plastic containers in our cooler. We would open cans of beans with the can opener we kept in our back seat and pour them over the quinoa. We got around the problem of silverware by pilfering plastic forks and spoons from coffee shops, or using coffee stir sticks as chopsticks (which, by the way, isn't very convenient). We also mastered the art of leveraging Sharaya's talent, offering bars and restaurants an even trade for dinner on the house.

When our friends in Everette returned home, we moved to an apartment right in the middle of the city where our friend Josh lived. He used to go to our church in Portland, and he had found out about our adventure on Facebook. His apartment was small, but he told us he would blow up an air mattress and that his girlfriend would come over and cook us dinner.

Getting our stuff up to his apartment was a little trickier since he lived on the sixth floor with no elevator, and there was no parking on the downtown street below. But we used the system we had already developed, and modified it a little. Sharaya dropped me off by the front door to wait with the luggage—two suitcases and two purses—and went to find a parking place. Twenty minutes and ten city blocks later, we both said a prayer that our car would be safe parked on the street overnight and asked Josh to ring us in.

Each day we ate meals with different people. A friend from my college invited us over for dinner, Sharaya's childhood friend cooked for us one night, one afternoon we ate lunch at the house of an acquaintance—a loose church connection who cooked steaks on the grill. Then, of course, there was Sean and Eva, who despite the fact that we had still not committed to be "Christian" or "non-Christian" artists, packed sandwiches and told us we could come pick them up—no strings attached.

One afternoon, while Sharaya sat in a coffee shop calling venues in Utah, I stepped outside to call Ben. It was the middle of the day, but there was just a chance I could catch him. I just wanted to hear his voice.

We talked and I told him about Sean's question and Eva's question, and how I couldn't get them off my mind. I spilled my guts about how I didn't really want to be a "Christian author" because I didn't want anyone to tell me what I could and couldn't write about, and he hummed in agreement.

"Whatever you do, please don't stop being you," he said.

It took several minutes to hang up after the conversation because of the weight of it, but once I did, I felt a sense of satisfaction settle over me. This was good. Good things were happening. We were only days into our trip, and I already felt fuller than I had before we left. *This is what it feels like to let go,* I thought.

Sharaya and I drove from Seattle to Spokane to Boise to Salt Lake City and then to Park City. From Park City we headed to Denver, then Colorado Springs, then Boulder. She played different shows with different people in each place, and each day we made new friends. We developed a knack for scouting out the best coffee shops in town, and mastered the art of ordering a single drink, sharing it, and staying for hours on end.

We stayed with different people at different houses, some of them old friends, some of them just generous strangers. But no matter where we were or who we were with, there was always Ben. Even just his name showing up on my phone was a comfort. They were just words, but words that seemed to hold a certain substance to them, so that if you put them in the trunk of your car they would slide around back there, clunking against the sides each time you turned a corner. If you set them on your chest they would feel all warm and heavy. If you dropped them on your toe, they would hurt, and possibly break a bone. They were weighty and important and, no matter where we were in the country, they were anchoring me home.

At night, before I went to bed, I would try to sneak out of wherever we were staying to call Ben. I would stroll around the neighborhood, sit on curbs, talk sometimes for a few minutes, sometimes for hours. Our relationship unfolded, all across the country, and I unfolded with it. It was a long, slow, sweet romance, incubated by warm weather and sudden rainstorms. We huddled under awnings together, hundreds of miles apart. We ducked beneath the the shade of thick trees to avoid the blazing sun.

There was a certain beauty to our distance, although at times it was painfully inconvenient. Our emotional relationship hung on words we spoke to each other. While there was no room on the road for physical touch, the highway opened itself wide for postcards, emails, and text messages. When I was tired, I talked to Ben. When I had a bad day, Ben could make it better. When I needed advice, Ben was always there.

5

roadblocks

"When we are no longer able to change a situation,
we are challenged to change ourselves."
VICTOR E. FRANKL

IT'S HARD TO FILL in all the blanks of the places we traveled, because a list does not do them justice. Every place had a personality, and friends along the way who treated us to coffee and couches and dinner. Every place had a feeling associated with it, a trail where I would go running in the morning, even a song we happened to be stuck on at the time.

There were the guys in Spokane who we met by chance, one of whom was the trainer for the Spokane Chiefs. I had a hip injury that was bothering me, and he did some sort of electroshock therapy to fix it. One night I sat outside the house, leaning against the brick and talking to Ben. I waited for a pause in the conversation before I asked the question I had been scared to ask for a few days now. "Does it bother you when we stay with guys?"

"I trust you, Ally," he said, and I marveled at his strength and grace.

In Boise, I was stuck on Sharaya's song about what it feels like to have a crush on someone—the not knowing, the excitement. We showed up late to Sharaya's show because we forgot about the time change driving east, but the room was packed and Sharaya didn't have any time to panic before she got on stage. That was also where we met Jackson, a friend of a friend back home, an outdoor expert who told us he would take us camping in the Grand Tetons sometime.

In Salt Lake City, we stayed with a friend's younger sister, who was living there while she completed her master's degree. She and her roommate opened their home to us, which I remember thinking sat on one of the cleanest and most beautifully manicured streets I had ever seen in my life. They shared their couches, their kitchen, and their French press with us. We sat tucked in their little breakfast nook talking about the goodness of God and the goodness of coffee.

The other thing I remember about Salt Lake City was the library where we spent our work day. I swear the whole building was made of glass, top to bottom, and you could look out of the elevator as you rode up at the millions of books on display.

It's strange the things that stick with you when you move from place to place quickly. In some ways you think you'll remember everything, that you'll come home from a trip and have the whole thing locked away and held tight like a box full of pictures, notes, and memories hidden under your bed. But the days pass, and before you know it you're a year down the road, and you didn't really decide what to keep and what to leave behind. The memories picked themselves. The ones you never expected to keep wiggle their way into the safety of that box, and the ones you hoped would stick around—the name of that girl you met in the coffee shop that day, or the park where you stopped to eat lunch and play guitar between this city and that one—fade away slowly. You're not even sure where they went.

From Salt Lake City we drove to Park City, unexpectedly, because Sean did connect us with his friend Peter there. Peter's wife, Jane, greeted us at the door with hugs and offered us tea right away. Peter wasn't there right now, she said, but he would be back later. She showed us the basement where we could keep our things, and asked if we would like dinner before Sharaya's show. In each place we gathered postcards—fifteen of them for our fifteen biggest supporters—and I would write notes to each of them about our latest travels.

Two brothers invited us to stay with them in Denver. They were friends of Sharaya's since high school, and the older of the two moved out of his room so Sharaya and I could share the private bathroom. In Colorado Springs, we climbed The Incline—a 1.2 mile staircase that gains over 2,000 feet in elevation and looks out over the deep red and emerald-green mountain view. We came back to our car to find a parking ticket, but we didn't care. The disappointment we felt over this mundane daily disappointment paled in comparison to the elation of being alive and awake and free to explore.

That's what I remember—that, and the way the squelching hot summer afternoon turned into a rainstorm in a matter of about thirty seconds. I had never seen anything like that before, and I leaned out the window to take pictures in the rain as we drove around Manitou State Park.

In Boulder, Colorado, we stayed with a perfect stranger, a girl who had connected with us through another friend on Facebook. We played a show in downtown Boulder that didn't finish until around ten, showed up as she was about to go to sleep, and left before she woke up the next morning. We were going camping.

And it was on the drive from Boulder, Colorado, to a campsite in Jackson Hole, Wyoming, when the car first started to overheat.

ASKING FOR HELP

We pulled into a Safeway parking lot to fill our cooler with hot dogs and chili, and to restock our ice supply, when the temperature gauge started to rise above normal. It was Sharaya who noticed it.

"Ally, is this . . . ?" Her voice started to trail off before she could say the word *normal*, but I knew exactly what she was thinking. She pointed to the gauge to the left of the odometer—the one with the little boat-looking icon floating on the waves of water. We both leaned our heads in close, squinting as we pondered the slowly increasing red handle. And as we walked into the grocery store we talked back and forth about whether or not we would need to buy a can opener to open the cans of chili, and whether or not we should be concerned about the car.

So we did what every self-respecting girl would do in our situation. We drove to the local auto-parts store, popped the hood, and stood there looking at the engine, hoping that either (1) someone would come to help us, or (2) we'd have some sudden, miraculous revelation about what was wrong with it.

After a few minutes a nineteen-year-old AutoZone employee came out to ask if we needed any help.

"Actually, we do," Sharaya jumped right in. "Thanks for asking."

Our temperature gauge was looking a little funny, she told him, and he followed her to the driver's side. He asked if we had checked the oil level—we hadn't. I showed him the green canisters we had stocked in our trunk, gifts from my mechanic friend who recommended the high mileage oil. He helped us put a quart of oil in the car (it was just running a little low), and within ten minutes we were on our way.

We drove away with hopeful anticipation and Michael Bolton blaring on the radio (because it was Sharaya's turn to pick) and felt like nothing could stop us.

When the car started overheating the second time, it wasn't as gentle as it had been the first. The little red lever didn't ease itself above the line as it had done before. This time, it catapulted upward. And this time, there wasn't a faint smell of burning. There was a giant puff of smoke that happened to match the dark clouds that were hovering on the horizon in front of us.

I hope this isn't foreshadowing, I told Sharaya, as we pulled to the side of the road where, of course, we had no cell phone service. Sharaya popped the hood and we both climbed out of the car.

Again, we both stood there staring at our smoking vehicle, not because we had any idea what to do with it, but because it was the universal sign of trouble.

Sure enough, within a few minutes, a white truck emerged out of the distance, approached us slowly, and pulled over.

Up until this point, the trip had gone pretty much as planned. We had booked shows in our destination cities ahead of time, and our bookings kept us on track. There was plenty of time to explore, but there was also always work to do—blog posts to write, people to connect with about accommodations, shows to promote—so that kept us yoked to cell phones and Internet connections. Each day we changed our locations, which meant a new coffee shop, a new group of friends, and a different set of linens—but we also learned that life on the road could really easily become just as routine as life at home if we let it.

At the same time there was this sense that everything could go wrong so quickly. The further we got from home, the crazier this whole thing seemed. Sometimes I would look at our bank account and wonder what on earth we were thinking—leaving home without enough money to fill our car with gas, to visit every state in the country. Sometimes at night, I would lie awake in the bed next to Sharaya and wonder how it was possible to know someone so well, and still not really know them at all—how it was possible that someone so close could still feel like they were a million miles away.

The more disoriented I became, the happier I was to have Ben. Even if everything went to pieces all around me, at least there was him. At least I could count on the fact that I could wake up every morning with a text message about how amazing he thought I was, or how he couldn't wait for me to come home. Even if everything else fell apart, I could look forward to talking to him, and seeing him, again.

The look on the trucker's face wasn't promising as he inspected under the hood of our vehicle, which wasn't actually smoking too much by now. Sharaya and I stood back and watched, waiting while he shook his head at our apparent problem. "It could be your head gaskets," he told us, and we nodded, as if we knew what head gaskets were. "Is that bad?" I asked, and Sharaya kicked me in the shin. "It's not good," was his response.

He offered to tow us to Laramie, Wyoming, where he knew a mechanic—the only mechanic within 400 miles, which meant we didn't really have an option. So we agreed. While I sat in the front seat of this stranger's car, squeezed up against Sharaya and listening to her carry on a conversation, all I could think was: *I told you so.* Maybe I was worried that's what people were going to say when we called them and told them what had happened, maybe I was saying it to myself. Either way, I couldn't stop thinking about how I was going to spin this to people so they didn't totally freak out—and so I didn't. Not long later, we arrived. Joe let us out, and unhooked our vehicle from his. We thanked him, and he waved goodbye.

Clouse was our mechanic, and he was from Sweden. He had moved to Laramie a few decades ago and had just sort of "gotten stuck," he explained. I didn't like the way he said that—"gotten stuck." He agreed to look at our car, but couldn't do it for a couple of hours, so he offered to drive us to the local coffee shop while we waited. That's what he usually did with out-of-towners, he said. *Oh great,* I thought. Something about the way he said "usually" and "out-of-towners" made me think this was not going to go well.

Gathering our things out of the car looked a little like a funeral procession: we did it slow and methodic, with cold expressions and no more movement than the situation required. We climbed into Clouse's VW bus, and I hoped this didn't suddenly turn into a scene from a scary movie.

"The mayor owns this place," Clouse told us on the way to the Black Cat Cafe, swerving in and out of narrow back roads. "She's in here all the time, usually behind the counter." Sharaya and I smiled and tried to maintain polite conversation as we jostled around in the backseat. We arrived at the coffee shop and settled in at a round table with our bags and purses and Tupperware containers full of lunch. I looked around and saw people glancing in our direction, and when I stopped to think about our pile on the table from their perspective, I stopped. I bet it looked like we were moving in for a few days. We had become brazen in our coffee shop takeovers in the past few weeks, but this was different.

"We're not homeless!" I pictured myself announcing.

At first, I didn't call anyone. I couldn't bring myself to do it. *Maybe the whole thing will blow over and we'll be on our way,* I thought. It would be so much easier to tell the story when it was a "funny thing" we experienced a hundred miles back. But now?

Now it was humiliating. And every time I thought of picking up my phone to call my parents, or to call Ben, I heard those same stupid words echoing in the back of my mind: *I told you so.* I couldn't bring myself to do it.

The coffee shop was charming for a town as remote as Laramie, Wyoming, and I had a latte sitting in front of me, which felt very luxurious for us right now. But after a few hours of waiting to hear from Clouse, the reality started to settle in that I was, at some point, going to have to tell people. Here we were, in the middle of nowhere. We didn't know anyone. We didn't have a working car. And we didn't have any money, or any place to stay tonight.

First we called Jackson, our new friend expecting us in Jackson Hole that evening to camp with him. He listened and explained how he'd already made the drive to Boise to meet us, so there was no point in going back now. He would set up camp and be there when we made it. *When we made it*—something happened in me when he said that. It was so small, but for some reason it meant a lot to me, to have someone assume we were going to "make it."

I wonder if this is what we all need—more than lectures about the places in our life where we might be failing or falling apart. More than finger-pointing and criticism, or even well-intentioned advice. I wonder if what we need, more than anything, is for someone to tell us we're going to "make it." No matter where we are in our journey, or what has gone wrong, I wonder if what we really need are people who are waiting for us, without judgment, willing to say, "Do what you need to do. I'll be here *when* you make it."

Next I called my parents. I told them what had happened, and my dad asked a hundred questions, most of which were about the car for which I didn't have any answers. My mom told me she loved me and she wished she could give me a hug. Then I called my sister and she said she was praying it wasn't the head gaskets, whatever those were. Then we sent out a mass text message to all of our friends asking them to pray too. I hovered over the "call" button next to Ben's number.

Sharaya and I talked about "worst-case scenario" while we sipped our lattes. But we talked about it the way you talk about a math assignment—with disinterest and detachment, as merely something in the way of your to-do list being accomplished. We could pay the money to fix the car, depending on how much it would cost. We could buy a new car. We joked about selling the car, flying to Hawaii, and calling the trip a wash. And, actually, the longer we sat there, the more that started to sound like the most enticing option to me. Sharaya looked up the price of used cars. I Googled "What are head gaskets?"

Meanwhile, another cafe customer had started talking to Sharaya. He had overheard one or the other of our phone conversations, and before I knew it Sharaya was telling Moon the whole story, and he was telling us not to worry. After all, this is how half the residents of Laramie had ended up here—because their cars broke down. And when he saw our eyes get wide he added, "If you need someplace to stay tonight, you can stay with me. Well, not me, because I live in a tent, but my friend has this couch—by the way, do you smoke weed?"

Before I knew it I was outside, on the phone with Ben, doing the thing I promised I wasn't going to do—collapsing into tears, explaining the whole situation, and asking for help. I stood around the corner from the Black Cat, turned toward a brick wall to hide the tears that, once they started, wouldn't stop. I pressed the phone to my face and told Ben I felt like a failure.

"A failure? Why do you feel like a failure?"

"I just feel like we took this big risk to come out here, and now I don't know how we're going to finish. What if we have to come home?"

"What if you *do* have to come home? Then what?"

I said nothing and wiped my tears.

"Then you did everything you could," he continued. "You took a brave leap, gave it everything you had, and you got to see more of the country than most people do in their lifetime. Besides, I get to see you that much sooner."

I smiled.

"You're not a failure, Ally. No one else thinks that. You shouldn't, either."

Before we hung up he asked me what I needed. There was that question again. *What do you need?* He had given me so much already, I felt bad about asking. But what we really needed was a place to stay tonight.

"Please don't make me stay with Moon and his friends!" I said.

"Don't worry," he said, "Everything is going to be okay." And something about the way he said it made me believe him.

Ben booked us a hotel. Clouse called to say that it was the head gaskets, and it would be $5,000 to fix. Sharaya suggested we go get our nails done.

"Sharaya," I said, incensed. "We don't have any money!"

"That's where you're wrong," she told me. "We have money, we just don't have $5,000."

As a stranger filed my nails and painted them a ridiculous shade of pink, I pondered how many shows we would have to play, and how many CD's we would have to sell to come up with $5,000. I wondered if people in Lararmie liked music, and how long it would take us to walk to the next city. How desperate would I have to be, I asked myself, to take Moon up on his offer?

For tonight at least, we had a hotel, thanks to Ben. In our room that night, Sharaya researched used cars and local car dealerships, and I went for a run—the only thing I knew how to do when I didn't know what else to do. Those times when there are options, but none of them seem like good ones. None of them take you where you were trying to go. None of them have the outcome you hoped for. You start to wonder, "What on earth am I doing here? Why did I come out here in the first place?"

I ran and ran, but I couldn't figure it out.

The thing about packing light is that, for better or for worse, you have limited options. Limited options can be frustrating, because you don't always get exactly what you want. But in another way, it makes your decision easier. You can't spend all day mulling over what to wear. You don't have that luxury. There is this shirt, or that one. The end.

I wonder if this is why packing light scares us so much, because we aren't sure we'll get exactly what we want. We're scared to choose anything—a school, a job, a spouse—because choosing one thing means letting go of several others. But sometimes having limited options is a blessing. It makes it easier to choose our path, and choosing means we get to zoom in and enjoy our one, complicated, imperfect path, instead of trying to halfway entertain a bunch of others. No matter which school we pick, it won't be perfect. No matter who we marry, our spouse will have flaws. But choosing means jumping in and accepting that path for all of its triumphs and trials. It means letting go of other roads, but in the end, it's better than never really choosing anything at all. In order to hold on to one thing, you have to let go of something else.

So the next morning Sharaya and I ate the continental breakfast at the hotel, which we turned into continental lunch and continental dinner by discreetly stuffing boxes of cereal and bagels into our purses. Then we drove my barely working 1999 Subaru Legacy GT on the shoulder of the interstate to the closest Subaru dealership in Cheyenne, Wyoming—thirty miles away. It was a long shot, we figured, but if we drove about twenty miles per hour and stopped every so often to rest the engine and fill the coolant, we could get there. And when we arrived, we could try to trade our Subaru in for a new car.

Miraculously, and two hours later, we did arrive. We pulled the car up to the closest parking spot, waltzed in the front door, and told the salesman what we were looking for: a used four-door sedan with low mileage and lots of cargo space. We told him we were looking to trade in our current vehicle. And four *long* hours later, we signed papers for a 2009 Subaru with 19,000 miles.

We had to co-sign to get the deal, since I was the only one with a current paycheck (I was still receiving checks from the school district through the summer) and Sharaya was the only one who had proof of residence (since she was subletting her condo back home). And while it certainly didn't follow conventional wisdom for us to finance a twenty-thousand-dollar car while we were traveling across the country without jobs or predictable incomes, we were on a fifty-state road trip, for heaven's sake. What part of our story followed conventional wisdom? Were we really going to let a little glitch like head gaskets get in the way of our epic road trip? I don't think so.

So we paid a small down payment—a fraction of what it would have cost to fix my car—and with the small, but not insignificant trade-in value for my old Subaru, we secured a fairly low payment on the new one.

Our salesman followed us out to our new car where he handed over the new keys and took the keys to the old one, which he laid eyes on for the first time since we walked in the door several hours before. We transferred our things from the old car to the new one with as much grace as could be expected for the amount of stuff that we had—a full cooler, a lock box on the roof, several suitcases, sound equipment and a clothing rack hanging across the backseat.

The trunk space was smaller, and the space behind the seats was a different shape than the old vehicle, so our system was skewed, but at this point it didn't matter anymore. We just sort of shoved everything in where it would fit. And when we had everything transferred except the parking ticket we had picked up in Colorado Springs, which we conveniently left in the glove box, we held everything in the back two doors with one hand, counted to three, and pulled our hands away at the same time we slammed the doors.

Several used car salesmen looked on in amazement.

So we cruised down the road to our campsite in Jackson Hole a day late and a few hundred dollars short. And I finally had the time to listen to a voicemail from my dad that said, very simply, "We're just reading your update, sweetie. Sorry to hear about your head gaskets. Whatever you do, don't buy a new car . . ."

DO YOU REGRET IT?

Sometimes I look back and wonder if we ever should have bought that car. I think about the poor salesman, going to start my old Subaru for the first time and realizing that something was seriously wrong with the head gaskets. I picture a plume of smoke rising from the hood as soon as the key is turned in the ignition. Sharaya assures me they don't care—they have technicians who can fix the car far less expensively than we could, that they make their money through trading cars just like ours. She points out that, if they were really concerned about the mechanical condition of our car, they would have had their mechanics look at it before they agreed to trade. She promises me we didn't do anything wrong. But—I don't know, something about it just makes me feel a little queasy.

It was one of those defining moment decisions. We had to make a choice—this way or that way—and our decision would impact both of us for a very long time. The choice we made in the car dealership that day would determine the destiny of the rest of our trip, and the rest of our lives. We've all had to make decisions like this. We've had to choose a place to live, or a job to take, or how to respond when someone does something awful to us. No choice seems perfect. Every decision has consequences. It feels impossible to know which way to turn.

So what about the decision we made? What about the consequences we chose? Was it worth it? Since hindsight is 20/20, everyone always wants to know how we view our decision in retrospect. Well, it depends on when you ask us, and what part of our story we're living at the time.

If you asked me that day, while I was speeding down the highway to the Grand Tetons for a three-day camping trip with little to no cell service, I would have told you yes. I could practically smell the campfire burning, practically taste charred hotdogs and toasted marshmallows, could practically feel the burn in my legs from squatting on a log to eat it all in the fresh, open air. We were free again. The road was open in front of us.

But if you asked me later, after our bank account dwindled, or after we had an argument so big I considered going home, or worse, after we arrived home and things didn't turn out the way we planned—the answer might have been different. This is why we can't measure the value of our decisions based on outcomes. Most of life is not an outcome. Most of life is unfolding on the road in front of us. The "outcome" can change as fast as the scenery.

Of course, there are right decisions and wrong ones. I believe that. Some things are quite clearly wrong or right, and if we decide to ignore the boundaries of right and wrong, we will pay the consequences. But sometimes there are not right and wrong decisions. There are just different choices with different benefits, different ramifications, and different baggage.

So I let myself wonder if we made the "right" decision buying a car that day, but I don't let myself obsess over it. Was it the prudent decision? Probably not. But was it the right decision? It depends on who you ask, and when.

Someday when I get to heaven I'm going to ask God about right decisions and wrong ones. I'm going to ask Him what He thought about us buying the car that day. I'm going to ask Him if He was ever worried about our credit scores, or our ability to pay our bills. I'm really curious to hear what He says. Until then, I'm not going to live my life based on fear of doing the wrong thing, making the wrong decision. I'm not going to be reckless, but I am going to give myself freedom to make mistakes. I'm going to give myself a free pass to mess up every now and then.

IN THE MOUNTAINS

We raced toward the Grand Tetons in our new car, fielding calls from friends and family members who wanted to make sure we had heard the stories on the news about the bears who were eating tourists and the ex-convicts loose in Yellowstone. We had heard the stories, first from our car salesman, and then from the television, and then from the various other phone calls that followed.

We thanked them for their concern, but told them that we would be okay. We were meeting a friend there—a camping expert we had met in Boise who, as soon as he heard about our desire to spend a few nights in the Grand Tetons, agreed to come with us for protection. In fact, we assured everyone, he was so committed to this camping trip, he'd been waiting there for more than twenty-four hours while we tended to our ailing Subaru.

Our airtight organizational system had broken down somewhere between the old Subaru and the new one, unfortunately. The trunk space wasn't the same, so the sound equipment didn't fit as well as it had before. The space behind the seats didn't fit our suitcases, so there were speakers in the backseat, and bags shoved in every nook and cranny. The passenger seat was pushed as far toward the dashboard as it would go, and I reached to the back, digging through our piles of stuff to find fruit leather and roasted almonds we could add to our bagels for lunch. I texted back and forth with Ben for a few hours, but as we neared our destination I told him, "We'll be out of cell service for the next few days." He texted back, "I'll miss hearing your voice."

We followed the directions our new friend Jackson had given us, which sent us through Jackson Hole and then onto winding, dirt roads, twisting and turning until we were high into the mountains. After thirty minutes, we pulled into a field overlooking a mountain range, where we parked our Legacy in a field of high grass next to his Forester and watched the sun set in front of them like a car commercial. "Here's a reason to buy Subarus," we joked.

We enjoyed all the luxuries that camping had to offer. We huddled around the campfire each evening and in our respective tents at night, disappearing inside of sleeping bags to stay warm. Although it was summer, the temperature drops at 6,000 feet when the sun goes down. We enjoyed the lethargic glow of each sunset and each sunrise, waking up not as our alarm clocks dictated but as the sun warmed our tents enough so we could emerge from our cocoons inside of them. Each morning we made the long, slow, glorious decision to enter the world. Even though, first, we had to master the art of changing clothes while sitting on the ground.

We ate all the weird concoctions that camping allows—even weirder at times than what we would eat on the road. We made macaroni and cheese but didn't have butter, so Sharaya used a smashed-up avocado instead. It looked green and disgusting, but tasted delicious, and we swore when we got back home we were going to eat it this way from now on. Camping does that to you—makes you think things you wouldn't otherwise think, eat things you wouldn't otherwise eat, and do things you wouldn't otherwise do.

Camping is strange like that. I mean, we basically leave behind all of our things for smaller, less luxurious versions of those same things. We take our mini stove, mini French press, mini bowls and plates and chairs. We take plastic silverware and our most rugged clothes. Then we drive to a place that is far, far away from our sturdy, comfortable houses and set up tiny, flimsy, cloth ones. We sleep on the ground inside of them, all the while eating freeze-dried food we cooked on our mini stoves. We skip showers, we squat to pee, and we call it recreation.

A special kind of simplicity happens when you leave behind all things unnecessary, and even some necessary ones. There is no noise, no chaotic motion—just silence. All of a sudden feelings start to rise to the surface you didn't even know you had. You start to think thoughts you didn't realize you were capable of thinking. There's an incredible clarity of mind that comes to you when you leave everything comfortable behind

As we were camping, I talked to God. The chaos of the previous days faded away, and the quiet pressed in, and so did Jesus. I guess that's what happens when we leave behind all of our extras to venture out into the big, wild, chaotic world. We find the One who made it, who made us.

It felt good to sit with Him, like it does to sit with a close friend. It felt comfortable, and the conversation flowed the way it would if we were sitting on a couch together, feet tucked up underneath us with cups of coffee in hand.

But it also felt overwhelming. All the feelings I had kept at bay in the past few weeks, hidden behind new cities, new friends, text messages, status updates, and blog posts suddenly came rushing over me. It was like looking in a mirror. I could see myself.

I was scared. It wasn't fair that I was scared. After all, what reason did I have to be afraid? God had provided for us. Every time we had needed something, our need had been met. We had never been stranded. But no matter how much I looked back, I couldn't help but be afraid of what was to come. Was God the kind of God to lead His kids toward disaster, without offering them a way out? He hadn't done that so far, but who was to say He wouldn't? Could I trust Him?

I cried tears of embarrassment as I told God I wanted to trust Him, I wanted to have faith that He was going to carry us through this journey, but I was having a hard time.

I looked out at the mountains and thought how they must have formed over hundreds of years, tectonic plates smashing into each other one big, painful push at a time. I thought about the earthquakes that must have taken place so I could sit here, enjoying the way these creatures, which were alive in their own way, were jetting up from the horizon. I wondered if life was like this. I wanted to make something beautiful, to be something beautiful.

As scared as I was of chaos and the unknown, I was equally scared of the mundane and predictable. In fact, I felt caught between the two. Which one was I supposed to choose? I was desperate for a road map, something concrete and definitive that would answer all these questions. At the same time I worried I would take all the right turns, make all the right steps, follow all the directions, and at the end would find out the terrain of my life was meaningless and boring. I told God all of this, and He just listened.

Sometimes His most important answers come in the silence.

I asked Him to help me discover what He wanted me to write about, in a way that acknowledged He probably wouldn't answer in any concrete sense. I prayed He would whisper words to me, and I promised I would commit them to paper. *Is that what it means to be a "Christian writer"?* I asked God. Because if it is, that's the kind of writer I wanted to be.

I want to be the kind of writer who is awake to the realities of heaven, but engaged in the realities of this world. I pictured myself throwing a lasso around the feeling I had right now, in the middle of nowhere, and dragging it with me back to civilization. That's what I hoped I could do with words. I hoped I could invite people into realities they had never experienced. I hoped I could wake them up to a life they wanted to be living. I would give up anything to keep this feeling—the feeling of being close to Him.

"That's packing light," I felt Him whisper, but it wasn't so much of a voice as it was a deep reassurance from somewhere inside myself.

I sat on that ridge and looked out over the mountains and, for the first time in my life, I realized God was for me. He was on my side. He wasn't trying to pull the wool over my eyes, or play some cosmic game of hide-and-seek. He wasn't trying to trick me into following Him. He wasn't trying to force me. He was here, He was available, He was pursuing me. And all the things I had worried about before—our bank account, our luggage, getting a new car, our credit scores—everything just started to fade into the background. Everything was going to be okay. I knew it. He loved me, He loved me, He loved me. That was all that mattered.

PACKING LIGHTER

Our camping adventure ended in the middle of the night, which might sound strange but comes with a perfectly logical explanation. Jackson had to be back to Boise to go to work in the morning, a drive that took a couple of hours, and we didn't want to be left alone to camp with the bears and ex-convicts. Besides, being the independent and self-sufficient women that we were, we weren't exactly sure how to properly take down our tent. So we woke up hours before the sun, packed our car by flashlight, and began our drive to Yellowstone National Park.

The problem was that the park was only an hour away and didn't open until eight. More importantly, no coffee shops were open, and we were exhausted. So we decided to pull into a rest-stop parking lot to sleep for a couple of hours until the town around us woke up. Sharaya was in the passenger seat, turned backwards in the fetal position—head by the dashboard, resting on a heap of things I couldn't identify in the dark. I was face first in the pillow I had shoved against the steering wheel.

The longer we lived out of our car, the more disorganized we became. Pillows, sleeping bags, clothing, purses, shoes, smelly socks, a haphazardly folded tent—our things were so carelessly shoved away that we didn't have the slightest clue where anything was. What had once fit so snugly was now in complete disarray. It seemed like our things had quadrupled in size since we'd packed them, and I'm pretty sure if you opened the door it would have all fallen out. Even worse, we smelled of sleeplessness and campfire and multiple days without showers.

I think life is like this. When we're just starting out, we think everything will become clearer with time. Decisions will get easier, life will become less confusing, everything will "fall into place." When I was in high school, I thought college would be where my questions were answered. When I left college, I expected the pieces of the puzzle to just "fit" after graduation. After college I kept waiting to get a job, buy a house, or get married. The pieces of the puzzle would start to fit then. But the longer I traveled, the more I realized things don't get *more* organized with time. They become less so.

And baggage, contrary to popular belief, doesn't just fall away if we forget about it or push it out of our memory. In fact, pushing things out of our consciousness is perhaps the quickest way to make a mess. Time doesn't heal all wounds. Time makes them worse. The only way to make sure we're packing light is to take inventory of what we have—over and over again—and always be willing to leave things behind.

We tried to sleep in that parking lot, but you could tell from our profound sighs of discontent that we were not experiencing success. After nearly a full hour, Sharaya sat up with that hazy, irritated "It's morning, don't bother me" look in her eye. Then, with a sense of fresh resolve and determination, she swung her door open, stepped out of the car, and opened the back door. She pulled the suitcase from behind her seat, pounded it resolutely onto the pavement (with a kind of middle-of-the-night aggression), and climbed back in the front seat. She pulled the lever on her right-hand side, and the seat flew backwards. She let out a deep, contented sigh.

I know I should have explained to her the dangers of leaving your suitcase in a rest-stop parking lot overnight, or been worried that she was taking up an extra parking space beside us, but I didn't. Instead, I blinked the sleep out of my eyes, looked around, and wondered silently why I hadn't thought of the brilliant idea before she had.

Without a word, I copied her movements—got out of the car, pulled my suitcase into the parking lot, and climbed back in. We leaned our seats back, and before we knew it, we were both snoring.

We woke up at seven to the sound of people outside, walking from the parking lot to a nearby restaurant. They were having a conversation with each other which stopped suddenly for one of the guys to say, "What's this? A yard sale?"

Sharaya went for coffee and a cardboard box while I unloaded the car.

"We're filling this whole thing," she said when she returned, dropping a three-foot tall box on the ground. "It's going in the garbage or going home."

"We're pleasant in the mornings," I said.

The decisions we made in the next ten minutes probably should have been unnerving. We were hundreds of miles from home and didn't have money to buy new clothes, or shoes, or anything else we got rid of if we realized we needed it later. But facts were facts. Everything just didn't fit. We had to get rid of some of it, and we were too tired to worry about our decisions. Instead, each decision felt remarkably unimportant. So we just started shoving stuff into the box.

Sharaya would hold something up. "Do we need this?" she would ask and I would shrug my shoulders. We kept our suitcases, our cooler, and most of the big stuff, but we sent home everything we figured we could live without—which turned out to be a lot. Then we took advantage of the public restrooms in a way that was new for us, brushing our teeth and washing our hair in the sink and attempting, albeit awkwardly, to blow-dry our hair under the industrial hand dryers.

Later, we would try to remember what was in that box, but we couldn't think of a single thing. We didn't miss any of it.

Maybe sometimes it's best to make decisions like this—without overanalyzing or overthinking. Some of our best decisions are made on the fly, on instinct—without too much deliberation, without an elaborate pro/con list. I'm not saying it's bad to think through things, but if we thought through all the potential hang-ups and holdups, if we pondered all the mistakes that we could possibly make, maybe it would prevent us from moving forward in our journey.

And perhaps that would be the worst mistake of all.

6

change your expectations

"Life is a collection of a million, billion moments, tiny little moments and choices, like a handful of luminous, glowing pearls. It takes so much time, and so much work, and those beads and moments are so small, and so much less fabulous and dramatic than the movies."

SHAUNA NIEQUIST IN *COLD TANGERINES*

WE LEFT YELLOWSTONE NATIONAL Park and headed north through Montana, over to North Dakota, and down to South Dakota and through the Black Hills National Forest—making sure to collect postcards along the way. The rolling hills and green trees seemed never ending, always brimming with hope and possibility of what could be over the horizon. We didn't have anywhere to stay in South Dakota, but we weren't worried about it. We had a tent, and it was still warm enough to camp, and we had our pick of 100,000 acres of national forest.

Sharaya drove most of the way, while I scrawled in my notebook. Carly Simon blared on the radio and every now and then we'd start to sing along (dramatically, of course). We stopped to get gas and filled our cups with coffee at the Travel Mart. There was a half of a container of yogurt left in our cooler, so we added dry oats to it, a sprinkle of cinnamon, and passed the container back and forth between us, sharing the same spoon, until the mixture was eaten.

Since we had left the city, cell and Internet service had dwindled and we couldn't always tweet our location, or post a blog, or interact with family and friends via Facebook. I couldn't even get text messages from Ben sometimes for hours at a time, so home started to feel even farther away.

Even so, the scenery couldn't have been any more grandiose. Sometimes it seemed like we had circumnavigated to another planet, or that this was some sort of green screen that someone was piping in. At some moments I would feel like life couldn't possibly be this spectacular, that a place like this couldn't possibly have existed for my entire life without me knowing about it. How could I have lived this long without knowing that somewhere, 1.25 million acres of trees were towering over scenic highways, shading them from the blazing South Dakota sun? How could my world have been so small?

Suddenly the hundred miles of winding road out in the Columbia River Gorge, the hiking trails back home I used to claim as my own personal playground, seemed like such a joke compared to here. These trees had been around longer than I had—by several hundred years. What made me think I was important? What made me think I mattered? The farther we drove from home, the more I seemed to shrink smaller and deeper into our surroundings.

In its simplest sense, I felt like this is what happens when we let go of things. We step out of our own reality and into God's. We realize the world is much bigger than we expected and that we are much smaller, and we start to see what a miracle it is that we get to be a part of it. We see that we aren't as big of a deal as we thought we were. That's what I realized as we drove, that I was just one person—one twentysomething person in the midst of this ecosystem that has been alive and thriving for ten times longer than I had.

In one sense, it's depressing to come upon our own insignificance like this. In another sense, it's exhilarating. I imagine it must be the way people feel who wander into the middle of a party. You aren't sure what is going to happen. You don't have control over the whole thing. But you get to dance, and sometimes there's cake, and at the end of the night you leave with good stories and a few new friends. That's where we stood in the middle of South Dakota. We still weren't exactly sure what God was doing, or how we were going to be a part of it, but we were curious. We were exploring. We were desperate to be a part of what was unfolding around us.

People would talk about how "courageous" we were being for taking a trip like this, and I happily accepted the compliment. They were right, in some ways. But I also thought about how we weren't being as courageous as outsiders might assume. I watched people at home have babies or start relationships or launch businesses and thought about how they were just as courageous as I was. Life is made up of moments, of tiny, little decisions that take us one direction or another. We had the same opportunities for courage that anyone did. My life wasn't inherently more courageous than anyone else's. I wondered if people knew that.

Sure, our lives were different. We ate breakfast out of plastic containers and never really knew where our next meal would come from. We slept on different sheets each night, sometimes in houses of people we were meeting for the first time. We accepted free food from strangers and took advantage of "all you can eat" anything. We took straws, napkins, and condiment packets from gas stations.

But in other ways, my life on the road was exactly the same as it was before I left. I did the same things every day that I used to back home, the same things all my friends were doing back in Portland. I woke up. I drank coffee. I ate breakfast. I worked. In some ways, the road trip made all of these routine rituals seem more exotic. Each night I was in a different coffee shop or cafe, meeting different people, selling CDs, and listening to Sharaya. But in other ways, it seemed like the road trip was just a new setting for my same old story.

I started to notice, gradually, that I had a hard time staying up past nine again. Sometimes I would stay up later so I could talk to Ben, or for one of Sharaya's shows, or because one of our hosts would want to ask us questions, but these slowly became the exceptions rather than the norm. I still liked to go for a jog every morning, so much that it would put me in a bad mood if I missed it. When Sharaya said or did something that hurt my feelings, I found myself ending conversations with her altogether. This was the same stuff I'd always done, even when I had lived in Portland.

And then I started to feel that at home, all this had been easier. Life is easier to control when you have access to more resources, and now that my resources were running low, I noticed how attached I was to things. I noticed how frustrated I became when I didn't get my way. And all of this made me feel like an impostor when people complimented my courage. Courage meant doing something different, didn't it? I wasn't really doing anything different yet. I'd given up everything I knew to give, and I still didn't feel the freedom I expected to feel. In fact, I lived in this tiny, little space in the cockpit of a car and, sometimes, if I was honest, I felt trapped.

Freedom is complicated. Sometimes the things we think will make us feel free don't. And sometimes the things we worry will pin us down are exactly the things that teach us what we wish we knew all along—that freedom is less about circumstance than it is about perspective.

THE PROBLEM WITH EXPECTATIONS

Deadwood, South Dakota, seemed to emerge out of nowhere, almost like it approached us instead of the other way around. It was dusk when we first saw brick buildings and cobblestone roads materialize out of the sea of green trees. Saloon signs hung low along the main drag and, although the town was quiet, you could hear a gentle buzz rising in the heat of the evening, like something exciting was about to happen.

We followed signs through the town to find a campsite where we could set up our tent before it got dark. We didn't know where we were going, and this would be the first time we had set up our tent on our own, but we didn't have any choice other than to handle it by ourselves.

It took us almost a full hour to find an appropriate campsite and to figure out how the whole thing worked. First, you pull into a designated campground, of which there are dozens. How you know the difference between each one, or know the best one to pick, I had no idea—and my only strategy for answering the pressing questions life threw at us recently was Googling it, which didn't work since we were still out of cell range.

Though if we had learned anything about camping so far, it was that all campsites are relatively the same except for one simple factor: proximity to the bathroom. Do you choose a campsite that is closer to the bathroom, for the sake of convenience, and risk the possible smell? Or do you choose one that is farther away, in order to protect yourself from the potential stench, and brave the long walk in the dark? These are the questions you deliberate over when you are spending your life on the road.

The office where you pay your fee for the site was closed by the time we arrived, and didn't open until the next morning, so Sharaya and I got to work assembling our tent in the last few minutes of daylight. We donned our headlamps and found our way to the bathroom (which we had decided should be an appropriate twenty yards away, as long as the wind didn't change direction). We changed our clothes, brushed our teeth, and headed to Deadwood to eat some dinner. As we got ready, I couldn't help but think about how strange this was—us putting on mascara in an outhouse bathroom, getting ready to go for a night on a "town" that probably had a smaller population than any place we had been so far.

When we arrived in Deadwood, it was a Friday night and the party was just getting started. Bars and restaurants were bustling with people and lights. The streets were alive. If I squinted, it almost looked like Portland. Take away the hipsters and their hipster music, trade them for Harley bikers and country music, and there was really no difference as far as I could tell. The buildings were just as charming, the crowds as fascinating, and there was at least an equal air of "We're cool. Why aren't you?"

All of the restaurants looked pretty much the same, with wooden signs hanging from chains outside their front doors, slowly rocking back and forth in the night air. We chose one that had music playing inside. When we walked in the door, it was clear we weren't the typical clientele. Everyone else in the restaurant, it seemed, was wearing leather, with their long hair pulled back into ponytails, and for the most part, everyone looked over the age of forty-five.

A country band was playing on the small stage at the back, and what little space there was between the tables and the stage was crowded with people dancing. Sharaya and I giggled as we watched middle-aged men and woman swing each other around like they were teenagers. One man in the middle of the dance floor, who may or may not have had too much to drink, was shouting, "God bless America!" in an Australian accent.

Deadwood, I decided, was a people-watching jackpot.

We ordered hamburgers and sat back, wide-eyed and smiling, taking in the scene. "Anything else I can do for you ladies?" our server asked.

"Yeah," Sharaya said, motioning to the room. "What is this?"

"It's the last stop of Sturgis—a motorcycle rally that travels through the country each year." Sharaya and I nodded at each other—that made perfect sense. He walked off to the next table, and we turned back toward each other.

"Is this trip everything you expected it to be?" I asked Sharaya.

"Not exactly."

"What's different?"

"A lot of things. I think you have an image in your head of how something is going to play out, and then later you look back and see how unrealistic that image was. But it doesn't change the fact that you had that image, and the real thing doesn't measure up. I don't know, it's hard to explain. I'm not saying this trip doesn't measure up."

"No, I think I understand." I paused. "So what was the image you had in mind for this trip?"

"I pictured us . . . I don't know, frolicking through fields, I guess," she said with a dramatic wave of her arms above her head (that was her frolicking impression, I think).

"Really?" I asked, laughing.

"Yeah. I guess I just didn't think about how much work it would take to travel across the country. I expected it to be magical or something."

"So are you disappointed?"

"Not disappointed. Just need to adjust a little."

"What do you mean by that?"

"I mean I don't think it's bad that I came out here with expectations. Having a plan isn't bad. I just have to be willing to adjust it."

Right then our server returned with our burgers and our conversation turned from expectations to the food that had been set in front of us. We stuffed ourselves with burgers and fries and, when we couldn't eat anymore, we leaned back against the booth, full and satisfied. Then Sharaya broke the silence.

"I think we should dance!"

And with that, we stood up and found our way to the middle of the dance floor where we stood with a bunch of people who were nothing like us—they talked differently, dressed differently, and each and every one of them had helmet hair—but we danced. We grabbed each other's hands and spun around, putting our full body weight into it so that if one or the other of us were to let go, we each would have gone flying in our separate directions. It wasn't frolicking through fields, but if you ask me, it was better.

After we paid, we left the restaurant and wandered in and out of the shops on the remainder of the street. We met a couple who joined the rally from New York City (it had been a lifelong dream of theirs), viewed the exact spot where Wild Bill Hickok was killed, viewed the other exact spot where Wild Bill Hickok was killed (apparently multiple restaurants and shops like to claim this fame), and then climbed back in our car to drive to our campsite. As the doors thumped closed we both sighed, wordless expressions of our exhaustion and satisfaction.

Deadwood was nothing like Boston, or New York, or Chapel Hill, all places we would enjoy over the next few months. But it was radical and unique. And as we drove back to sleep in a tent, I thought about what Sharaya had said about expectations. It made so much sense. So many times in my life I had gone into a situation with expectations about how it was going to be, expectations that later left me disappointed. Maybe what I needed wasn't fewer expectations, or lower expectations, but the ability to adjust them in the middle of my trip.

"New road rule," said Sharaya as we wound over the curvy mountain roads in the dark. "Anytime there's danceable music, we dance!"

We slept poorly and coldly for very few hours and woke up cranky with kinks in our neck. We broke down our tent in silence and loaded all of our things into the car. The minute we turned the key, we also cranked up the heat and pulled out of our campsite toward the office—which still wasn't open, so we still couldn't pay our fee. Sharaya sighed and shook her head. And as we pulled a U-turn in the parking lot, she whispered, "Coffee."

Later, when people asked about my favorite stop of the trip, I would always come back to Deadwood. It wasn't an easy question to answer. There were as many places to love as there were places we had visited, each of them for a different reason. But I think it was the way that Deadwood came out of nowhere that made it so memorable for me. There was something about the way it emerged out of the cracks of South Dakota, a place I had written off, a place I had assumed was just desolate and boring, that made it feel significant. I wasn't expecting Deadwood. I don't know what we were expecting, but this wasn't it.

People say you shouldn't have expectations for things because your expectations will just be disappointed, but I don't think that's true. I mean, I see what they're getting at, but a life without expectations? That doesn't even seem possible. Besides, it might look at first glance like it was my lack of expectations that made Deadwood memorable, but I think there was more to it than that. More exciting than the "surprise" of Deadwood was the way the experience helped me frame the rest of our trip. Deadwood taught me to expect more, not less. Deadwood was a symbol of how exciting everywhere else *could* be. If a place like Deadwood exists in South Dakota, what might we find in Iowa, or Vermont, or upstate New York?

We all have Deadwoods we run into every now and then. We get a new job, or go to school, or even get married, thinking this is going to be one way or another, but then things don't turn out as we'd planned. Our expectations are disappointed, or at least confused. Maybe we expected something wonderful, and instead it's terrifying. Maybe we were expecting it to be difficult but rewarding, and instead it's just plain hard. Maybe we were expecting to frolic, and instead we're talking about head gaskets. Sometimes it can feel like our expectations are letting us down. Sometimes it can feel like they're just throwing us for a loop. But maybe it isn't our expectations that get us frustrated and confused. Maybe it's our inability to see our "Deadwoods" for what they are.

Deadwood wasn't a disappointment. It was a symbol of hope and a promise of uncertainty, if we were willing to see it that way. It was a reminder that we never know what is coming, so we should always expect more than we're expecting. In a world where it's too easy to let the scenery start to blend together as it flashes past,

Deadwood seemed to say: *Anything is possible.* So the problem with expectations, if there is a problem, is that our expectations aren't big enough to hold the possibilities that will unfold in front of us. Our single perspective is so limited.

Vision changes everything. Sometimes we need to change locations in order to see something amazing, but sometimes it's simpler than that. Sometimes what we need is to change our perspective. It's not about ignoring expectations, or lowering them. It's about letting the events of our journey shape our expectations, even as they shape us. If the location where you're standing is less than energizing, check your vision. Don't abandon your expectations. Try to see them from a different perspective.

Maybe if we mastered the art of expecting the unusual, we would start experiencing the unusual. Maybe we have more control over the direction of our lives than we think. Maybe we should live our lives in a constant state of expectation, always curious and excited about the possibilities that could unfold in front of us. Maybe it is our sense of vision that colors our reality.

WHEN EXPECTATIONS ARE DISAPPOINTED

The morning started to look up once we had our coffee, as post-coffee mornings do. We were still in sweats with our hair in messy sleep buns, and we hadn't showered in a couple of days, but we were on our way to see one of our most anticipated sites of the trip—Mt. Rushmore. Plus, we were laughing about the fact that we had just abandoned our campsite without paying. I asked Sharaya what it was called when you camped somewhere illegally. She didn't know. "There's a word for it. I know there is!" I said, and thanked God we had cell phone service again so I could Google it.

Sharaya called her friends in Omaha to finalize details for what time we would be there, and we checked three gas stations before we found South Dakota postcards. I texted Ben: "Don't tell the authorities . . . but I think we might have just inadvertently squatted (that was the word!) in the Black Hills National Forest."

It was only about an hour from our stop at the gas station to get coffee to Mt. Rushmore, and the time passed quickly. We suddenly rounded the corner and there it was, right in front of us: the object of all our expectation and anticipation. Mt. Rushmore, off in the distance.

"It looks smaller," Sharaya said.

"No kidding."

The road wound around back and forth, and every now and then you could see the faces of Rushmore peeking through the peaks of the trees. I had expected to get chills at the sight of it, like you do when you experience the culmination of something you've waited for your whole life. Like the first time you tasted chocolate ice cream, or the very first step in Disney World. I had expected to be overwhelmed with sights and sounds and lovely sensations—the art and history of it all.

Instead, the whole thing fell sort of flat. Mt. Rushmore was far smaller than I had expected, first of all, and the natural beauty of the peaks and surrounding fields were cluttered with vendors selling touristy gimmicks—T-shirts and mugs and postcards for the absurd price of a dollar apiece (thank goodness we thought to stop earlier—otherwise, South Dakota postcards would have been "lost in the mail" on the way to our supporters). In fact, when we saw a sign that said "Parking $20," we looked at each other, eyebrows raised, and decided it wasn't worth it.

It was so disappointing, especially after a city like Deadwood, to have an experience where something we had hoped for and waited for was so clinical, so manufactured. Sharaya rounded a bend and pulled over on the side of the road. "Get out," she said—not in a mean way, but in a way that said, "I'm taking control of this situation," so I did. "Smile," she said, grabbing my camera and continuing her economic instructions. I obeyed, then looked behind me. Sharaya had framed Mt. Rushmore perfectly in the background.

"All right," she said, handing me back my camera. "Lunchtime?"

It's always been funny to me that Deadwood, a place we knew nothing about before our trip, would remain such a place of interest while Mt. Rushmore, a historic landmark I've wanted to visit most of my life, would be such a disappointment. There are a thousand reasons I can think of. Maybe it was because of the rawness of Deadwood, and the way Mt. Rushmore was cold and commercialized. Maybe it was all the pictures we had seen of Mt. Rushmore before we saw the actual thing. Maybe it was just that there wasn't anything to look forward to anymore. Maybe we missed something at Mt. Rushmore because we hadn't taken long enough to look around. Maybe we gave up too easily.

Either way, I don't want to stop having expectations just because I might be disappointed. I can't guard myself against every kind of heartbreak.

But maybe the healthiest way to form expectations is to expect less in the specific and more in the general. Just expect amazing scenery, without knowing what it will look like it. Don't try to imagine it, just know it will come. That way, when it comes and it looks different than you expect, you won't miss it.

Expect a town like Deadwood, even if you don't know where it will pop up. Expect success, even if you don't know where it will come from. Expect love, even if you don't know who it will be with.

Then, when disappointments come, don't assume you did the wrong thing. You didn't. Don't ask yourself how you could have avoided it, even if you see an obvious answer. Avoiding pain is not the point. Ask yourself who you're becoming. Because at the end of it all you'll have thrills, and you'll have disappointments, no matter which route you took. But more than that, you'll have you—the one who is breaking forth and unfolding to become something new.

THE PROBLEM WITH RULES

After a while, it doesn't matter who you're traveling with—they just start to get on your nerves. When you live in close proximity to someone, you see them for who they really are, not the person they project to the rest of the world. It's funny how we all do this. Every single one of us. We hide all the little, quirky things we do, as if no one is ever going to find out.

Sharaya, for example, is the lightest sleeper I have ever met. She can't fall asleep without a face mask over her eyes so the room is completely dark, and a little white noise humming on her iPhone. It's not what you would expect from someone like Sharaya—someone so fun and full of adventure—but it's true. If she doesn't have those two things, she'll toss and turn for hours trying to get comfortable. You would expect that from your grandma, or your English teacher, or anyone with your typical Type A personality, but not from Sharaya.

The other thing about traveling with Sharaya was how serious she was about packing the suitcase. Our system had changed again, somewhere along the way, so that we only had to take one suitcase into a house with us each night. It made sense. But Sharaya had this specific way of folding the jeans so that you could see the back pockets at a quick glance, and a certain place she wanted the workout clothes so that they didn't touch the other things. It was so important to her. If I packed the suitcase wrong, she would unpack it and pack it again.

But Sharaya wasn't the only one with quirks. I had a hard time closing containers the whole way, for example. Not just some containers—every container. I wouldn't close the milk all the way before I put it back in the cooler, which wasn't a problem until you picked it up and milk spilled everywhere. Spilled milk leaves a really pleasant smell in your car, in case you weren't aware. Even after she brought it up to me a couple of times, I couldn't seem to close the shampoo bottle so that it didn't spill all over everything.

Several times I heard her call my name from around the corner, and I would know what was coming. Sure enough, she would emerge a few seconds later, hand on her hip, holding just the corner of our ziplock bag dripping with shampoo. I would wince. I had done it again. It was the strangest thing. I didn't know I did this until she pointed it out, and I couldn't figure out why it was so hard to stop.

I also had a tendency to make noise just for the sake of making noise, which couldn't possibly have made Sharaya more frustrated. If I had a pen in my hand, I would click it (even though it was against our rules). If I was chewing gum, I would smack it. If I was eating a bowl of cereal, my spoon would perpetually clink against the side. It wasn't even a conscious thing. I wasn't doing it to annoy her. But that almost made it worse. I would start making noise without even realizing it, swirling my glass with ice, staring at it from above, fascinated at the way it moved around the cup. Then I would see Sharaya staring at me, out of the corner of her eye.

"Sorry," I would say, bashfully.

She would let out a long, deep sigh.

The other thing was my inability to sleep in in the morning. No matter where we went, or how late we were up, I would wake up around five, hours before she was ready to get out of bed. I would read, or write, or go for a run, but since we were sharing a bed, and sometimes an air mattress, it's no wonder that this caused problems for us. Combine this with how difficult she found it to sleep, and with the fact that she was the *opposite* of a morning person, and let's just say the tension was building.

We arrived in Kansas City to the sound of storm warnings. We drove straight to church, for no other reason than it was Sunday morning, and we were following our road rules. Someone had recommended a particular church to us, so we looked it up ahead of time, got directions, and found out the service started at eleven.

Sharaya drove and I navigated, which was problem number one.

Problem number two was that in order to get to church on time, we'd had to leave Omaha at seven, which meant getting up at six. Did I mention Sharaya isn't a morning person?

And problem number three was that we'd stopped following our own rules, one by one. We hadn't ignored all of them, obviously. We were going to church that morning. But the ones about praying together every morning and being honest about how we were feeling—those rules we had just sort of pushed to the side when they became too inconvenient, embarrassing, or complicated.

We never decided to quit following the rules, but that's usually how it goes. It starts with one decision. You're too tired, or too frustrated to do what you said you were going to do, so you take the easy way out. It doesn't seem like any big deal. It's just one day, one time, one tiny little instance where you're going to do what is easy, instead of what you know is right. But over time those decisions add up, and before you know it you're way off course from where you were headed.

That was what happened to us. We never decided we were going to stop affirming each other, or praying together, or being honest. It was just that life got in the way, the way it always does. This is the way it works when we're at home, working our regular jobs. It wasn't any different on a road trip.

Despite these problems, we were on our way to church. I was dictating directions, except, for whatever reason, we weren't communicating very well. I would say something, and she would misunderstand. Or, I would tell her to turn right when I really meant to turn left. Every once a while I would think we were in one place when we were really in another.

"You can't trust the blue dot!" She snapped at me, referring to the tiny GPS dot that was supposed to show you your exact location on the map. More often than not, we were learning, it was just plain wrong.

And because I was tired, I let my insecurity do the talking. *She always thinks she's better than everyone at everything,* I told myself. *No one can do it as well as she can.* I thought about how she was always correcting me and telling me I was doing it wrong. It didn't matter if we were picking a movie, or packing the suitcase, or navigating our way somewhere. She could always do it better than I could.

Fine, if you're so good at navigation, I thought to myself *you can figure out the directions for yourself.* I put my phone in the center console and looked out the window. She looked at me, waiting for me to yell or say something rude, or at least be honest about how I was feeling.

"If you're mad at me, just tell me," she said.

But I wasn't going to talk to her. It was already decided. I didn't care if it was in the rules or not. If she was going to snap at me, I was going to disappear. She couldn't stop me. Things would be less messy this way if I just shut her out.

I could have come up with a perfectly noble explanation for my silence. We were on our way to church, after all. No need to start a fight now. I could have made it sound like I was defusing a conversation that might have gotten ugly. But really I was just scared. I was scared to start the conversation because I wasn't sure where it would go. We should just both suck it up and go to church, I figured.

The worst thing happens when we keep quiet about our insecurity. It starts to fester and grow. It seems reasonable, logical even, to keep it locked inside. We can make a really convincing argument for ourselves. But ideas that would be revealed as ridiculous the minute we said them out loud start to make sense when they play over and over in our minds. *Maybe she's right,* I thought to myself. *Maybe I can't be trusted to give directions or do anything else. Maybe I never should have come on a road trip. I am ruining it. I know it, she knows it. It would be better if I just went home.*

Sharaya pulled up to a four-way stop and pulled the emergency brake. It was a standoff in the car, unlike any we had experienced up until this point. We sat at a stop sign. My phone sat in the center console. It all lasted about thirty seconds, which always seems longer when you're in the heat of the moment. Then, as if on cue, two faint female voices emerged out of the distance.

At first, they were so quiet I wondered if I was hearing things. But the closer they came, the more real they sounded, and by the time I saw the two girls to whom the voices belonged, there were two more. Then there were five. Then ten. Then twenty, not just women but men, all parting like the Red Sea around our car, all carrying Bibles under their arms. We followed the crowd upstream, until we saw the building.

It was an old church building, but the people emerging from it weren't old at all. In fact, most of them were our age.

"Is this the church we were looking for?" I asked out loud.

"Does it matter?" Sharaya said.

We inched our way up the narrow back stairs to the sanctuary, and took our seats in the crowded pew. For several minutes in the silence before the service began, we didn't say a word to each other. I looked down at my bulletin and read about Bible studies that particular church hosted, and what series were coming up. Then, I just said it.

"I told you we'd make it to church okay." It was quiet, under my breath, and if you hadn't known the context, you would have thought I was being optimistic. I guess that was sort of my point—to slam her while I had the chance, to really give her a jab when I knew we were in a place where she couldn't fight back. I'm not saying it was right, but I was hurt, and hurt usually comes out as anger, and anger can make you do strange things.

"Are you joking with me right now?" Her voice was cold and sarcastic.

"Nope."

"You're ridiculous," she whispered.

We spoke quietly, back and forth until our conversation turned into a full-blown argument. Right there, in church, in a pew, we clubbed each other with our words.

"I can't believe we're fighting in church!" Sharaya whispered.

"Oh, like we'll ever see any of these people again," I said.

The pastor went on to talk about compassion, and loving one another as much as we love ourselves, and we each half listened, if only to distract ourselves from our own fuming, and then found our way back to our car. We didn't look at each other. It was minutes before Sharaya finally broke the silence.

"It seems like you're really angry, Ally."

"I am," I said.

It was the first time I realized it, saying it out loud, but I was. I had followed the rules, after all. Okay, maybe not all of them, but the major ones. I had come on this trip, even when I was afraid. I had bought a new car without a noticeable panic attack. I felt like counting out my accomplishments on each of my fingers, congratulating myself for being so strong.

Every night, at Sharaya's show, I stood by the merchandise table, faithfully and responsibly attending to my job. I told strangers how amazing Sharaya was so they would buy her CD. Then I told Sharaya how amazing she was so she could get on stage and sing. But even after following all the rules, I felt empty.

I listened to myself talk and as I did I realized, here I was again—this same old place. Sure, I had given up everything to come on a fifty-state road trip, but I was still the "rich young ruler." I was still asking, "*What more* do I have to do to get to *heaven*?"

The problem with rules is that they don't protect us like we think they do. Sometimes they don't protect us because we don't follow them, sometimes they don't protect us because we become obsessed with them, and sometimes they don't protect us because they were leading us in the wrong direction all along. Some rules are ill-advised, and we just keep following them blindly.

Sometimes we stop following rules because it's just easier. It isn't an angry or rebellious thing; it's just a convenience thing. It usually happens one day at a time, one experience at a time, one decision at a time. We just make what seems to be a single isolated decision—"just this once"—not to follow our conviction. We know we should talk to that person, or go home early, or tell the truth when it hurts, but it's just easier not to. We don't want to ruffle any feathers or make anyone upset. We don't want to step out of our comfort zone. But single decisions add up over time. They become habits and patterns.

That's what had happened to Sharaya and me. We stopped following some of our rules because we forgot, or life was moving too fast, and we just lost sight of the vision for why we had established them in the first place. Both of us had developed bad relationship patterns.

Sometimes we stop following the rules out of rebellion. This is why I didn't talk to Sharaya before church, even though we had agreed to be open about how we were feeling. I felt controlled by her frustration with me, and the only way to regain control was to rebel against this simple rule: talk about it. If I chose not to talk about it, I had control again, didn't I? I can still picture myself, sitting in the front seat of the car, refusing to talk to Sharaya or help with directions. The thing I hoped would bring me freedom was stealing it from me instead. That's how rules control us even when we don't follow them.

Sometimes we don't ignore the rules, but we become obsessed with them. It had happened to us in little ways. I felt like such a nice friend, such a dutiful person standing at the merchandise table every night. The encouragement I gave before she stepped on stage started as a gift, but over time it became an obligation. Without realizing it, Sharaya started expecting it from me, and I started expecting something in return. That's what happens when we get too attached to rules. We feel gypped when we don't get what we were hoping for.

This happens in life all the time. We serve at church, or volunteer at a local charity, or reach out to someone in need. We do it not because we're concerned about the people who need the resources we're offering, but because it's the "right thing" to do and we're obsessed with being right. Suddenly, it becomes more about us than it does about them. It's the reason we throw baby showers and make meals for people who are in need and it's the reason Sharaya and I woke up so early to go to church that morning, honestly.

We do what we're "supposed" to, just because we're "supposed" to do it, and it makes us feel good for a minute, but ultimately it leaves us frustrated and angry. It doesn't give us what we're longing for. Sometimes I wonder if it's better to break rules and stay humble than it is to get on our pedestal and follow them.

Maybe we should have skipped church that morning, so we could have talked to each other, looked each other in the face. That was the objective, after all, wasn't it? To preserve the friendship? If the rule wasn't protecting the friendship anymore, why were we still following it?

I wonder if, many times, rules are pointing us in the wrong direction.

Rules give us a false sense of control. They make us feel like if we just follow a list of instructions, we're sure to get the outcome we want. We do this in so many areas of our lives. We have a set of rules for our faith, our sexuality, our marriages, our dating relationships, for choosing a church—nothing is off-limits. We tell ourselves to *always* do this, and *never* do that, and everything will turn out perfectly. Worse than that, we back up our rules with Bible verses and tell everyone else to follow them too.

"If you want a good life . . . " we tell ourselves, and everyone else, "you better follow this set of guidelines."

But the rules never buy us the safety we think they will. Go to church every Sunday, trade off music turns, don't click pens. Just follow this list of arbitrary things and you'll get a great trip. Life isn't like that. Friendship isn't like that. There are no formulas or recipes with guaranteed results. Rules are just rules, not relationships.

When Sharaya and I focused too closely on the rules, we stopped focusing on the friendship. We stopped thinking about what was best for two unique people, with two unique needs, in a very unique circumstance. We stopped looking at the situation with our own discernment, making our own, informed decisions. The rules took precedence over the person. Rules make everything seem too easy, or too difficult.

When it comes to rules, I hope we never stop asking ourselves what the intent is behind the rules we're following, and if they're accomplishing the objective. I hope we don't become blind followers. Blindly following rules won't get us the reward we think it will. That's what the "rich young ruler" was doing—blindly following rules so that he could achieve some sort of reward at the end of it. If you're doing that, I think you'll find yourself feeling like he did, like we did that day at the church in Kansas City—like you're doing everything you can, and still missing something really wonderful.

As we talked, the whole thing started to unravel. But something had shifted. We talked about it not because we were "supposed" to, but because she cared about me and I cared about her, and this is what two people do who care about each other. They listen; they try to understand.

I admitted my feelings were hurt by the way she talked to me in the car. But it went beyond that. I told her my frustration had been building for a while. She explained how she was tired. She hadn't slept well in several nights, and it was difficult for her to get a good night's sleep at all. She woke up easily in the middle of the night, and easily in the morning. She wasn't used to sharing a bed with someone. As we talked, the tension released. We didn't fix everything right there in that conversation, but it was progress. It didn't have anything to do with rules. It was just two people, willing to get into the mess, willing to take responsibility for their part in the story.

We need a generation of people who aren't rule-followers—who aren't rule-breakers, either, but rather live lives that aren't dictated by the rules at all. Think about it: how much more engaged in living a good story would we be if we weren't blindly following the rules? How much more in tune would we be with the twists and turns of our journey, and prepared to handle them with conviction and grace, if we didn't think the "rules" were protecting us? We would have to pay close attention, exercise discernment, ask people to help. We'd have to let go of some rules that everyone else was following, and follow some that no one else was embracing.

Blind obedience isn't enough.

What would happen if we were willing to ask ourselves the hard questions and decide, over and over, what "rules" we were going to follow and why? What would happen if we asked ourselves, who came up with these rules anyway? What were they trying to accomplish with these rules? Is it a noble objective? Why are we following them? Are my motives pure?

Until we stop blindly following rules, we're sleepwalking through our life. We become just like the "rich young ruler," who by all outward accounts lives by the rule book. Yet we still find ourselves saying, "What else do we have to do to get to heaven?" Perhaps if we lay our rule book down, we could hear God whisper back: "I'm right here, and there's a whole big, refreshing, frustrating, and satisfying world in front of us. Will you put down your stuff and come enjoy it with Me?"

7

when you don't pack light enough

"You gotta give up to get what you want."

MICK JAGGER

LEAVING SOME OF OUR rules behind, we found we traveled
lighter. We drove up through Iowa and Minnesota, over to Wisconsin, down through Illinois, then to Indiana, then back to Illinois because we forgot postcards, then through Indiana again
and on to Michigan. The baggage of our unspoken resentments
for each other no longer weighed us down. We played a putt-putt
golf championship with friends of mine in Wisconsin Rapids, and
Sharaya performed on a college campus where she experienced
one of her best turnouts yet. The university housed us in an open
room in a fraternity house, and I complained on the phone to Ben.

"It smells so bad in here!" I said. "I refuse to take a shower."

He laughed at me and told me to get some sleep.

We pulled our warm coats out of the back of the car and officially decided it was too cold to camp anymore.

We could feel the seasons turning, and we were turning with them. I pictured each of my teacher friends going back to school, and all of the students who had once been "mine." I wondered what I would be doing if I were home. I pictured the street where I used to live and how the trees seemed to explode with orange and yellow this time of year, and how days became long and stayed warm in Portland. I thought about pumpkin lattes and other luxuries we had left behind.

Then Ben and I talked about taking a trip together for Christmas.

"Mexico?" he asked.

"You're serious!"

"I'm serious. My whole family is going. Would you come with me?"

"Of course I'll go with you! We'll be back in time."

Of course I would go with him. We would be back in time. But taking a trip together was a big deal. The farther away we traveled, the more serious things became with Ben, and the more difficult it was to be away from home. Our relationship, which had at once seemed daring and bold, now ached inside of us.

I wanted him to meet my family. I wanted to meet his. I wanted to be there for parties and weddings and for a Tuesday night making dinner. I couldn't stand the thought of him being alone, or being with someone else.

To make matters particularly tense, we arrived in Ann Arbor and still didn't have a place to sleep.

The bank account was looking low and our car was feeling fuller and fuller, though it seemed we could never find anything we needed. I was keeping a list of things that had disappeared since we left Portland and it was growing: curling iron, computer cord, sweater, book, black dress, scarf, headband, etc. Our cooler, which we had once packed ritually every day with snacks and meals, and cleaned regularly so that food wouldn't get moldy and make our car smell, had become a bigger hassle than it was worth. When you get to someone's house who you've never met, do you ask them if you can bring your giant cooler inside to rinse it out? Do you ask them if you can use all of the ice in their freezer to fill it up? So somewhere in Illinois, we gave it to some girls who had given up their bedrooms for us. They went camping often, they said, and it would be useful to them.

"I hope we meet people who will feed us," I said as we drove away.

"We will," Sharaya said. "We're headed south."

But tonight, since there was no cooler, very little in the bank account, and no shows booked for several days, we decided we were going to have to learn the art of busking.

"This is so awkward," Sharaya said as we walked down the streets of Ann Arbor with her guitar in hand.

"No, it isn't!" I tried to be encouraging, even though I wasn't sure if it was awkward or not. "Trust me," I said. "You have such an amazing voice, people are going to love you, just like they do in every cafe, every restaurant, and every bar we've ever played in." She looked skeptical. "Trust me," I told her. "I'm the one who sees the expression on people's faces when they buy CDs. They are going to love you. They're going to be handing us money in no time."

I hoped I was right.

It took half an hour to find the "perfect" spot, a process which included Sharaya taking mental measurements of the distance between other loud sounds. She took into account any loud music coming from other restaurants and bars, the approximate number of people who were walking down our side of the street as well as the opposite side, and the likelihood that traffic would increase throughout the night by checking hours on the doors of storefronts around us. "This one closes at five," she would say. Or, "That's way too early. This part of town won't even pick up until then."

"I think you're just stalling," I told her.

We finally settled on a spot. With her guitar case open in front of her, she opened her mouth to sing, and at first she was right— this was kind of awkward. But I tried to keep things upbeat and positive. She sang a couple of covers to start, and then one of her own, and I think I might have given her a thumbs up at one point. It didn't matter if this was awkward. We didn't have another choice. We didn't have money for a hotel tonight.

Then, just as Sharaya's patience was about to run out, people started to gather. It started small, with a girl who was on her way to work down the way, and an older couple going to dinner. They heard Sharaya's voice and stopped. They would sit on the stoop or stand in a doorway and whisper back and forth to each other while she sang. Two men with coffee cups stopped on their stroll, leaning against the storefront behind her and listening.

Her voice, simple and sweet, wafted through the streets the way the fresh scents of a bakeshop do—with just enough of a taste on the wind to entice you closer. People who wouldn't have otherwise passed by couldn't seem to help but alter their course and linger for a minute or two.

Listeners would drop change, or a dollar bill, or, if they were generous, a five dollar bill in the open guitar case before they moved on. Each time a new wave of people passed, Sharaya would whisper to me and I would gather the funds in the guitar case so that there were only coins and a few dollar bills left. She had a theory about this. There was a fine science to how much money you left in the guitar case. It couldn't be too much, so that people would think you were greedy, but it couldn't be so little that they would think, *I wonder why no one else is leaving money . . .* Sharaya was sure that if we could strike the perfect balance, we could increase the odds of our listeners' generosity.

Sharaya sang a song she wrote called "Rush" about when you're ready to commit to love, but the other person isn't ready yet. When she got to the chorus, she sang, "If you would just hurry up . . . I would follow you anywhere," and for some reason, this time, it caught me differently than it had the dozens of times I had heard it before. It occurred to me how lucky I was to have Ben—someone who was ready to love me at the same time I was ready to love him. I thought about how rare and amazing that was.

I reached for my phone and texted him: "I hope you know how much I care about you." I had just tucked it into my back pocket when Hannah walked up.

She had stopped to listen, briefly, on her way to work. She had expected to listen to a song or two, but she hadn't expected to be moved like this. When she approached me she was in tears.

"I have to have that song," she told me. "My fiancé—" she said, "he's in the hospital right now. I'm not sure if he's going to make it. He's made a lot of mistakes, but he doesn't deserve to die like this. If he would just choose me . . . I would follow him anywhere."

She seemed so young, tucking her blond hair behind her ear, her complexion flushed and innocent. She was dressed simply in black pants and a white shirt, her uniform for work at the sandwich shop down the way. "If he would just pick me," I heard her saying, over and over again. I didn't know her full story, but I did know it was filled with heartache. "It's called 'Rush,'" I told her, and handed her a CD.

"Oh, I don't have any money," she said.

"Don't worry about it." I shook my head.

She stared at me, like she couldn't tell for a moment if I was serious, and told me that if we needed dinner when we were done, we could walk down to the sandwich shop and she would make them for us for free. I told her that sounded like a good trade.

"I know this isn't what you pictured," I whispered to Sharaya between songs, as I grabbed money out of the guitar case, "but let's not lose sight of what's happening right here. You're touching people with your music." She looked down at me and smiled.

"If you're wondering what you're called to do," I told her, "this is it."

In case you're wondering what to do with your life, this is it. First, you start with something you love. If it's singing, great. If it's writing, awesome. If it's playwriting or playing the trombone or developing video games, even better. Maybe for you it's just hanging out with people, making them laugh or feel really good about themselves. Then, find someone in need, someone who is hurting or living without. Find someone who, like the "rich young ruler," feels a sense of restlessness, like there has to be more, and just give them a taste. You don't have to muster it up, or muscle it out. Just do what you're good at. Just be the best version of you.

If you can't think of anyone, or don't know anyone who is hurting or in need, that's okay. Get started anyway. When you're doing what you were made to do, hurting people will come to you. That's what Jesus did. He just acted like Himself, and weeks after the start of His ministry, hurting people began to flock to Him.

When you are living in your passion, people around you who were once sleeping will be woke up. That's how you know. When we become who we were made to be, we come alive, but the people around us come alive too. Listen carefully. Watch. Are people responding? Are they changing? When we become who

God meant us to be all along, we leave a wake of His presence behind us.

Where your passion meets their need, that is your calling. And you might just find it where you least expect—in a Midwest town where you're broke and busking, where what you at first thought was awkward turns into a beautiful confirmation of what God made you to do.

After darkness had settled and the coffee a kind passerby had given us had lost its warmth, Sharaya and I decided to call it an evening. We counted our money—eighty-nine dollars. Enough for a hotel room. So we called the Holiday Inn and wandered down the street to eat a sandwich—compliments of Sharaya's most recent fan. Warm drinks. Dinner. Hotel room. It was all so simple, but it was exactly what we needed.

There is something beautiful about the way God provides when we need Him to. Most of us don't live like this—down to our last dollar, playing a guitar for money on the side of the road—and even if we do, it doesn't last long. We might think it's customary or even cute to be cash-strapped while we're in college or for a specific season while we launch a business or something, but ultimately we're striving for something "better." But what is better?

We pack our bags and our houses full of things we need. We fill our fridges and our cupboards. We fill our bank accounts and our budgets. Then, we make plans for how to make those houses and bags and budgets bigger so we can fill them with more things. We never want to be without. We always want to be prepared. But I wonder if we ever notice how much our expectation for bigger and better is weighing us down.

I wonder what would happen if we weren't so prepared for every possible circumstance. Would we really be deprived like we think we would? Or would God surprise us? Would He abandon us? Would we go without?

I used to think that being unprepared was the worst possible offense to God, but I've since changed my mind. Because when I don't have resources, I'm learning God often gives them to me. The lighter I pack, the more I realize He knows what I need even more than I do, and He is more generous than I ever imagined. Sometimes He even meets needs I didn't know I had.

SMALL COMFORT

We were settled in the hotel room, warm and comfortable, when Sharaya finally listened to a message that had come through earlier while she was playing on the street. I watched her face melt from disbelief to sadness and back to a blank expression before she pulled the phone away from her ear.

It was her condo. She'd been living there since the day she moved to Portland five years ago. She'd picked out the chandelier above the dining room table, hosted dinner parties, and thrifted everything from antique mirrors to a spare piano bench to make it hers. You could have learned a lot about Sharaya by wandering around her apartment.

This happens with homes. We put ourselves into them.

We invite our friends over, and they share about first loves in our living room and breakups in the kitchen over sizzling stoves. They get dirty footprints in our entry and leave rings on our coffee table and spaghetti stains on our carpets, and even though we think about how we should probably get it cleaned, we never do. It reminds us of them, and the home we've built and filled.

"My renter fell through," Sharaya said. "I have to be out of my apartment by the end of the month."

I watched the weight of grief and regret settle over her, and I knew how she felt. I thought about how houses weren't just houses. They were like relationships. They're where we unfold ourselves and unwind ourselves and where we become ourselves—the real version of us—the first-thing-in-the-morning, up-late-working, sick-as-a-dog, movie-watching, crying-in-a-heap version of ourselves. Slowly but surely, our places become a part of us.

"We're in this together," I told Sharaya. "What can I do? How can I help?"

I spent the evening trying to reach our friends back in Portland to ask who had a truck, and if anyone would be willing to coordinate the whole thing. Sharaya was embarrassed, and sad, so I told her I would take care of it. I was happy to do it. I called Rebecca and asked her if we could move Sharaya's furniture into our apartment—well, her apartment. I called my parents and asked if they could spare any space in the garage.

I put out an SOS on Facebook and asked for manpower. Then I watched as dozens of friends, some from our house church, some we barely knew, and some who had warned us that a trip like this might not be a good idea, volunteered to help.

At midnight, when it started to border on being too late to call people on the West Coast, I phoned Ben.

"You'll never believe my day," I said.

While Sharaya watched *Friends* in our modest hotel room, I ventured into the hallway, sat on the floor, and told him the whole story.

"So let me get this straight," he said when I finished. "Sharaya lost her apartment, and you've spent the last two hours calling your friends to move her furniture?"

"Yes."

"Why?"

"She's done so much for me. I guess I feel like this is one small thing I can do for her. Besides, this is what friends do. They take care of each other. They share resources. They take turns picking each other up and dusting each other off."

There was a pause on the other end of the line, and for a minute I started to feel insecure. Suddenly he sighed.

"I love you, Ally. I've been wanting to say that for a long time now, but it's true. I love you."

Then the words that had been on the tip of my tongue and the edge of my heart for weeks, growing and becoming something new and alive all on their own, finally broke ground.

"I love you too, Ben."

I didn't sleep much that night.

Part of what makes it hard to pack light is that often you think you're already doing it. Most of the time it feels like you're already living at bare minimum, like you've given everything you have to give. Sharaya had already sold her car, after all. She had gotten rid of all of her silverware, cookware, and luxury bedding. She'd given away most of what was in her closet, including dozens of pairs of shoes and expensive dresses. She'd already gotten rid of anything that wouldn't fit in the space of our backseat. What more was she supposed to give up?

I had done the same thing. I had taken all the risks I was "supposed" to take in order to come on this trip. I'd given up my apartment, my job, and pressed pause on my relationship with Ben just as it was beginning. But sometimes it takes a crisis—in your life or in someone's close to you—to realize there were all these little ways you were holding back. For Sharaya, it was her condo. For me, it was insecurity. It was keeping me from a deeper friendship with Sharaya, from embracing experiences to their fullest, and from a richer relationship with Ben.

Lying awake that night, I decided my insecurity had gone on long enough. I thought about how strange it was that when you let people into the smallest spaces and secret places of your life, you begin to feel what they feel. When they're sad, or angry, or tired, you become sad and angry and tired too.

This is how love takes shape. And as I drifted off to sleep, I melted into the reassurance that Ben loved me. He loved me and I loved him. There was so much safety in that—safety enough to leave my fears, insecurities, and doubts behind. Packing light had never felt this good.

LIVING THE DREAM

Boston welcomed us with open arms. Zooey, a girl we had never met but who happened to know a friend of a friend of a friend of Sharaya's, agreed to host us for the five days we were planning to be in the city. It wasn't until we were standing on her doorstep, pillows in hand, that I thought to ask, "How do you know Zooey?"

"I'll tell you later," Sharaya said with a laugh. "It's a really long story."

Without much fanfare, Zooey invited us in and showed us where we would be sleeping. She had a daybed and a pullout in the living room, each of which she had prepared with fresh sheets for us. She had laid towels at the foot of each bed. She showed us the refrigerator and invited us to help ourselves to anything we needed. "I'm headed to class, but let me know if you need anything at all," she finished. She left her cell phone number for us on the counter.

Unlike the other cities where we had played, we had four full days in Boston before Sharaya's only show, which gave us plenty of time to work, explore, and invite people to come. We ventured to Harvard, where we wandered around campus and tried to feel really collegiate. We joked about walking in and joining a class just like Rory from *Gilmore Girls*. We made friends at a coffee shop and invited them to come. We busked for a few hours and handed out Sharaya's card. We met a childhood friend of mine for lunch one day, and went to dinner with a guy Sharaya used to know. We followed maps for the underground train, accepted directions from strangers, and went everywhere on foot like tourists.

We had dinner with a friend of a friend from back in Portland. His name was Nick, and Sharaya had once been friends with his cousin, or something like that. He also went to Zooey's church, which we didn't discover until we mentioned his name to Zooey. The world can be so big and little at the same time. He took us to an Italian restaurant where we ate pasta and told him our story, and he said he would be at Sharaya's show on Thursday night. Then on the drive home, we tried to convince him how Boston was a great city, but Portland was even better.

We sat in a coffee shop for a whole afternoon, cleverly disguised as college students, working on press releases and bookings in Savannah, Charlotte, South Florida, Oklahoma City, New Mexico, and Phoenix. Instead of buying bagels from the coffee shop for lunch, I pulled fruit and crackers out of my purse, and a small container of cream cheese we spread using coffee stir sticks. We used about ten of them before all was said and done, because they kept breaking. Such were our meals on the road: unconventional, using whatever was on hand.

We invited the baristas to come to the show on Thursday, and when a guy asked to join our table, we invited him too. I wrote a couple of blog posts, one about kayaking the Atlantic and eating lobster for the first time in Maine. Then I wrote another post about what it looks like to lean into something, even when you're scared of it. I wrote on the back of forty-five postcards, playing catch-up from Ohio, Maine, and New York. The whole day was this beautiful collision of normal and magical and silly.

I was committing to something, or trying to at least, but with a kind of abandon that felt memorable and important.

"This must be what it feels like." I smiled at Sharaya.

"What what feels like?" she asked.

I thought about it for a minute. "Living your dreams," I said.

YOU'RE MISSING IT

On a night that happened to be Rebecca's birthday, Sharaya and I video-chatted with a group of friends back home while they moved Sharaya's furniture from her Pearl District condo into Rebecca's apartment in the suburbs. Jimmy had offered his truck, and Heather coordinated volunteers. Matt and Anna and Charlie and Liam lugged every item down the hall, into the elevator, out to the truck, and all the way across town.

"I can't tell you thank you enough times," I told Rebecca. "Tell everyone else we said thank you too."

"I have to say, these are the biggest birthday gifts I've ever received," she chuckled as a giant leather couch floated past the screen behind her.

Seeing our friends there together, without us, made the distance from home feel bigger now, like an elastic band stretched from there to here that kept getting tighter with each mile we traveled. We weren't even in the same time zone anymore. And on top of all this, my favorite season in Portland was coming, and I'd be lying if I said I didn't feel tugged west. I wanted to watch the leaves change with Ben. I wanted to drink cider and curl up on the couch, watching movies with my toes tucked under him for warmth.

Still, somehow, there was this overwhelming sense that there was purpose in all of it. I hadn't had that before, but I had it now.

The distance between Ben and me felt bigger and bigger, but somehow I knew the payoff was getting bigger and bigger too.

We drove to Rhode Island, bought fifteen postcards, and watched pink clouds melt into the Atlantic Ocean like cotton candy on a hot sidewalk, in all its fast-spreading pink.

On the way home, I texted Ben and told him I missed him, and that I couldn't wait to come home.

"Look at that!" Sharaya exclaimed as the ocean flashed in and out of the houses to our left. "You're missing it!"

And she was right.

LIKE JUMPING OFF A WATERFALL

Sharaya's Boston show was at a venue called The All Asia Cafe, which, contrary to its name, was neither a sushi restaurant nor a karaoke bar. We got ready at Zooey's house, curling our hair with the new curling iron someone had given us back in Wisconsin, and pulling clothes we hadn't worn in weeks out of the car. We put in a little extra effort this time, put on a little more makeup, maybe because this felt like a big city show, maybe because we hoped to see some people we knew, maybe just because we hadn't really dressed up in a while and we wanted to feel beautiful. We checked ourselves in Zooey's full-length mirror in the entry, loaded everything into the car, and drove to the venue.

We followed our usual routine: checked in with the bartender, ordered a drink, ran a sound check, set up the merchandise table. And then, like usual, Sharaya started getting nervous.

But something was different this time. It wasn't anything about the venue, or about Sharaya, or the set list she scribbled on a napkin as we waited. It was about me. Something had changed. Something had shifted.

I reminded her how much people loved her music, and how even though she got stage fright every single time she did this, the outcome was always the same. She always stepped onto stage beautiful and confident; she always amazed people with the sound of her voice and depth of her lyrics. I reminded her that she was strong, that she could make anything happen and overcome any obstacle. Even as I spoke I felt it. I had always meant the words I said as I coaxed her onto the stage, but today—I didn't know, something was better, something was new.

"Remember when I almost didn't come on this trip?" I asked, and then told her the story about the dream I'd had about the waterfall jump in Costa Rica the night after I told her I couldn't come.

"I think this whole thing is like jumping off of a waterfall. It's exhilarating and dangerous, and a little bit scary. Every time you get up on stage you'll feel it again. But I don't want to spend my whole life looking over the edge. At some point you just have to hurl yourself off."

Even as the words came out of my mouth I could feel something opening up in me. I could feel myself flying through the air and loving every minute of it.

"It is kind of like that," Sharaya said, smiling.

And from then until seven thirty when Sharaya stepped on stage, there was no time to be nervous due to the steady stream of people walking through the door, filling the tables and standing around talking to friends. Some of them were people we had personally invited, like Nick or my friend Sarah from Portland, and some of them had seen the flyer hanging where we'd placed it around the city. Many of them were friends with Nick, or friends of friends, or Facebook friends, or baristas we had invited on the fly. Sharaya usually played to a room full of strangers, but tonight there were so many familiar faces in the crowd.

Normally, I would have assumed my seat at the merchandise table and sat there for the remainder of the night. But not tonight.

Instead, I talked while Sharaya played. I greeted every familiar face. I listened as they told me their stories. I was on my feet all night amidst the crowd, instead of my usual post sitting in the back. Hours flew by, and before I knew it, it was midnight.

The whole time my phone was in my purse, which was hanging on the back of my empty chair. It was ringing and ringing and ringing, but I didn't hear it.

8

the things you have to leave behind

"This is the middle. Things have had time to get complicated, messy, really. Nothing is simple anymore.... Disappointment unshoulders his knapsack here and pitches his ragged tent."

BILLY COLLINS IN *ARISTOTLE*

DISTANCE TESTS ANY RELATIONSHIP, and just like any test, it proves a measurement of something—of quality or strength. It serves as a gavel coming down on its value or nature. And the physical distance between Ben and me, as well as the emotional distance that grew as I chased the direction I knew was right for my life, tested us and what we were building together.

On one hand, I had never sensed my passions and purpose so strongly. I was living life and writing about it. On the other hand, I was falling in love with someone who was waiting for me to come back home. It was like there were two things on opposite sides of the country that were calling my name. Each required passion, attention, and love. But there was also a limited quantity of those things to go around. And as the miles increased between us, I tried to make sense of it all.

The day couldn't have been more beautiful as we drove from Boston to New York City. I read Bill Bryson out loud and Sharaya and I laughed together. Then between essays we would sit in silence, looking out our windows at the view of the leaves changing, the flicker of sunlight warming our laps. Her Boston show success the night before made us both excited for the three shows she had booked in New York City. I could feel the energy building around what we were doing. We were gaining momentum, and it felt good.

It was a big, messy puzzle we were putting together—one of those 5,000-piece ones—and we were finally starting to see the big picture on the box come together. Each day we would work on different sections, and I would start to see shapes and figures form. Some days were better than others, but no matter what kind of day it was, I was starting to see how each day fit into the bigger picture.

Sometimes multiple pieces would blend together—the way they do when you're working on a section of sky or a tree—so that you couldn't tell exactly what piece belonged where. Sometimes you would have to labor over those sections for hours to discern where each piece went. But even when that was the case, after a while you would step back and start to see the full image unfold. The vision starts blurry, but after a while it begins to clarify, and what was unfolding right in front of us was friendship, passion, adventure, careers, and even love. What had been a million mixed-up pieces before was now slowly transforming into a beautiful picture—and it was gratifying.

I was thinking about Ben as we drove, because the night before when I talked to him after Sharaya's show, he seemed more distant than usual. It might have been because the miles between us were increasing. Or maybe it was because I had three missed calls on my phone before I was able to return his call. Maybe it was something else altogether. I sat on the stoop outside Zooey's apartment, watching people wander by throughout the course of our conversation. Our words wound inside and outside of theirs, and I'd sometimes pause for minutes at a time until the footsteps passed. I moved from the stairs outside her front door to the sidewalk, to a walk around the block, with my right hand holding my phone to my ear and my left tucked inside my shirtsleeve to stay warm.

I was telling him about the show. I told him how all those people had come, and about how excited we were.

"This is really happening. Things are really happening," I told him. I was so excited and waited for him to catch on to my enthusiasm. But he was quiet.

"How has your day been?" I asked, hoping to tilt the conversation in the other direction.

"Pretty boring," he said. "I met my neighbors today."

"Really? That's nice."

"Yeah. I think we're going to go to dinner tonight."

I didn't ask any more questions, probably because I was cold, and it was nearly two in the morning, and I figured I should get back inside so I didn't keep Sharaya and Zooey waiting to go to bed. But as I was falling asleep that night, I started to kick myself for that. How insensitive could I be? The least I could have done would be to ask him for more information, the way he always did for me. Were his neighbors men? Women? A couple? How had they been introduced? What did they do for a living? Why did he bring it up? It must have been important to him. I wondered if he was trying to tell me something. I chastised myself for not being more engaged, and at the same time for being too concerned, for hovering, for worrying too much.

Everything would be okay, I told myself. I would apologize and explain, and we would have a great conversation about it tomorrow.

But now tomorrow was here, and I hadn't heard from him. I had a bad feeling about this. It all seemed very strange and sudden. He hadn't texted me in the morning, the way he usually did. My head was spinning with doubts. Was he just tired? Had I caught him on a bad day? Was there something else I was missing? Or was I just reading too much into all of this? I tried to calm my fear with logic. I went through possible scenarios in my head. I knew sometimes he worked from home on Fridays, and I was three hours ahead of him, so maybe he was still sleeping. But noon his time came and went, and then one, then two, and I knew he wasn't sleeping anymore.

I texted him and waited—but nothing.

There was so much irony in our distance. It was Ben's strength and encouragement that had pushed me to be here, and my own sense of adventure that had attracted him to me in the first place. He was the one who gave me the courage to run the direction I had always wanted. It was Ben's love that made me feel safe enough to jump in *all the way*. But it was precisely jumping in all the way that seemed to pull me further and further from him. I was, without a doubt, becoming the best version of myself. But now there was a new question rearing its ugly head: Was the best version of me the right person for him?

I wasn't yet ready to answer it.

THE BIG APPLE

Our New York City accommodations fell through at the last minute. A friend from Portland said he knew a guy, who happened to know a guy, who had just been in a wedding with a guy who lived in New York. His name was Gus. At this point, these connections didn't even surprise us anymore. Our friend offered to call Gus for us, and sure enough, a few hours later he called us back and it was settled: this guy we'd never met would let us set up our mattress in his apartment, for just a night—or maybe two—until we could find another place.

We were so thankful we scribbled down the address; we didn't even think about where it was in the city or how risky it was to stay with such a distant connection—someone we had never even spoke with on the phone, who happened to be a guy. We did, however, laugh at the hilarity of our connection to him. "How do we know you again?" we would joke with Gus the whole time we were in the city. We decided to call him our second friend, four times removed.

When we arrived at his apartment, we pulled into the valet zone of what looked like a fancy hotel. Traffic buzzed by us on the street, and we were mesmerized by all of the colors, the people, and the doorman who rushed to our car to help us unload. I waved him away, telling him it was okay, we didn't need help. I didn't want his help out of sheer embarrassment more than anything else. Our car was a total disaster—stuff was everywhere, and we didn't have any idea what to bring up and what to leave behind.

Our once-carefully-plotted system was moot at this point, partially because nothing was where it was supposed to be anymore. If we took our one suitcase upstairs, there was no telling what was going to be in it. For all we knew, it could be food and socks without their match, or a few shirts but no pants. It was a disaster.

We were also a little bit concerned with theft, since we'd be parking our car on the streets of New York City. But even more than that, we wondered what Gus, who didn't have any idea what we were doing traveling to all fifty states, would say when we brought handfuls of loose belongings up to his nice, Upper East

Side apartment. We dug through piles of blankets and grabbed shoes, one at a time, until we each had our favorite pairs. Sharaya rushed to choose outfits from the clothes hanging on our rack, and we hoisted our suitcases out of their secure place between the front and back seats. Meanwhile, the doorman waited politely and loaded all of our things onto a hotel cart.

"We'll be right back!" we told him as we rushed away to park the car.

When we came back, our ramshackle pile of treasures was waiting for us, and so was Gus, in his fitted, V-neck shirt and thick-rimmed designer glasses. Sharaya stuck her hand out first and introduced the two of us.

"Welcome to the city," Gus said. He had one arm on the side bar of the hotel cart, the other in the pocket of his skinny jeans.

Gus ushered us inside, introduced us to Frank, the bellhop, and took us up the elevator to his apartment. Needless to say, from the moment he opened the door and let us in, we didn't feel particularly motivated to find alternate living arrangements.

Maybe it was the prime location, or the fact that we felt cool saying "Evening, Frank," to the doorman each time we came or left through the polished revolving door. Maybe it was the comfortable mattress (he had us use his, since it was nicer) or the even more comfortable couch, or the showerhead in the bathroom that had the circumference of a ceiling fan. Maybe it was the sheets Gus let us borrow that had more threads than we could count. Maybe it was the huge floodlight windows or the big-screen TV or the hardwood floors—I don't know. Maybe it was the way Gus suggested, within the first ten minutes of our arriving, that we go to a cast party that night for the movie he was shooting, or how he offered to register us both for the 5K he was running the next morning, honoring those who died in the events of September 11. Whatever it was, Sharaya and I both silently decided that we weren't going anywhere.

So we made ourselves at home. We unpacked our food into his cupboards, hung our clothes in his closet, and at one point I counted nine pairs of shoes lined up against his living room wall. We plugged in our electric toothbrush in his bathroom, and then because we felt at least a little bit guilty for the way we had totally taken over, we bought flowers and put them in a vase on the counter.

At night we would come home after our exploring, kick off our shoes, and say, "How was your day?" trying to distract him from whatever football game he was watching. We were hopeful Gus liked us as much as we liked him. But it wasn't until three days into our five-day stay that Sharaya and I sat over Thai food nervously trying to decide if and how we should break the news. We had given up our search for another place to stay. We started to lay out our excuses, but Gus simply looked at us and said, "It's okay. I realized pretty much immediately that you girls weren't going anywhere."

IS VODKA OKAY?

Gus worked on movie sets, and had been living in the city for a couple of years. Currently, he was working on a film with Jim Carrey. In fact, he told us the first day, there was a cast party happening that night. "I was thinking of going," he said. "Do you girls want to come? Maybe Jim will be there."

"Jim as in Jim Carrey?" I asked.

Gus looked at us, straight-faced, as if he hung out with celebrities all the time—which, for all we knew, maybe he did. "Maybe," he said.

Sharaya and I resisted the urge to squeal like a couple of starstruck teenagers and jumped up to start getting ready, dominating

Gus's bathroom with our makeup bags and curling iron. "This means we want to go, Gus!" I yelled at him from the bathroom. "In case you didn't catch that." I wrangled a particularly difficult strand of hair in the grips of my curling iron.

"We'll have your bathroom back to you any minute!" Sharaya yelled.

Just then my phone rang, and I knew it was Ben. The look on my face went from excited to heartsick. My excitement for the evening plummeted into worry. I dropped the strand of hair I was holding, only half-curled.

"I'll be right back," I said to Sharaya. And I felt my stomach drop as I stepped into the hallway to take the call.

"Hey," I said, trying to keep quiet. "Where have you been all day?"

"Sorry," he replied. "I got caught up doing some work stuff." His words were short, stilted. And I could hear noise in the background.

"What's wrong?" I asked him.

"Nothing," he said. "It's just been a long day." But I didn't believe him.

He asked what I was planning to do that night, and I told him about meeting Gus, and his apartment. I started to tell him about the cast party and Jim Carrey, but I could tell, if only from the lack of response, that he wasn't interested.

"What's wrong?" I asked again.

"Nothing," he said. "Let's talk tomorrow."

"Okay," I told him, even though it wasn't.

If he wasn't going to talk, I didn't know how to make him change his mind, so I hung up the phone and paused in the hallway to collect myself. *Don't cry,* I told myself, *just don't cry. There's no point. He said he had a bad day. Just trust him.* And when I felt ready to put on a smile, I stepped back into the bathroom and picked up where I left off. "What are we talking about in here?" I asked, since Gus was leaning against the bathroom door.

"About running a 5K tomorrow morning," Gus said.

I laughed.

"Sorry," I told him. "It's just that running is not exactly Sharaya's favorite pastime. Especially if it happens in the early morning."

"This run sounds cool!" Sharaya protested. "It's in memory of those who died in the September 11 attacks. Tens of thousands of people run. I can get into stuff like this."

"I'm already registered," Gus continued, "and I have an extra registration. I'd be willing to pay for a third one if you girls are interested."

"Why do you have an extra registration?" I asked.

"It was for my girlfriend," he said, looking at the floor. "We broke up."

"Let's run," I said.

"Yes!" added Sharaya.

"All right," he said, "I'll make it happen." Then he vanished around the corner to let us finish up.

I didn't hear from Ben for the rest of the night. Usually, he would have texted me to tell me he missed me and couldn't wait for me to come home. But my phone stayed silent and still. I wondered about it as we left the apartment, and as we walked down the street. I felt the weight of his absence on my shoulders, on my whole body, as we climbed into a cab. I felt it when we entered the party, and two young women, dressed in black and as beautiful as you'd expect them to be, greeted us at the front door.

"Name?" they asked us.

"They're with me," Gus said, and ushered us in the door.

The weight followed me. It sunk into the pit of my gut and followed me while we sat at the table. I checked my phone. A girl sitting next to me introduced herself. I tried to keep a steady "nice-to-meet-you" face on while we introduced ourselves. I checked my phone again. The guy sitting to my right ordered table service.

"Is vodka okay with you?" he asked. I paused. I wasn't sure if vodka was okay with me. First of all, an evening sitting around a table drinking shots wasn't really my kind of event. Second of all, I wasn't sure how much it would cost. We had some money in the bank, but not enough to be spending money on extravagant extras. But with everyone else at the table drinking, and with Ben's absence weighing me down, I suddenly lost all will to say no, even to vodka.

"What the heck," I said. "You only live once, right?"

"Right," he agreed.

The vodka was served to the table as a bottle, and he started mixing drinks. He poured the first round into shot glasses and passed them around the table until there was one sitting in front of everyone. Sharaya and I looked at each other and shrugged before we played along, drinking up with the rest of them. The next round he mixed with a variety of things—cranberry juice for some, tonic for others, soda water for me.

As I sipped on my second drink, I scrolled through my phone and thought about Ben. What was going on with him? One hour passed—no word. Another hour passed—no word. And when I looked down in front of me I realized my drink was empty again. I tried to remember how many that was, but counting was too hard. Instead, I opened my phone and sent a text to Ben. Conversations were happening all around me.

"What's up with your friend?" I heard one guy say to Sharaya.

"She's lovesick," Sharaya whispered back to him.

"Lovesick?" he hollered over the top of the crowd. "What's the point of being sick over love? You're wasting your time!" And they lifted their glasses in a sort of toast to my pain. The conversation continued, the commotion grew, and the bottle of vodka traveled around the table again and again until it slowly disappeared.

Hours later, when we were hailing a cab, my phone was still silent. We made it all the way home, in spite of the fact that I couldn't see very straight anymore, and settled onto our mattress on the floor. When I put my head on the pillow, I checked my phone one last time: 4:38 a.m. And the weight that had followed me all evening finally won out, and I fell asleep.

The reason rules don't protect us is that "rules" presume that every circumstance, and every person, is identical. When it comes to alcohol, Christians want to talk about the rules. Is it okay to drink? How much can I drink? Can I have more than one drink at a time? How often? Where is the line? On one hand, I see the concern. We've seen the damage that can come from failing to draw boundaries around something as powerful as alcohol. But in my experience, blindly following the rules when it comes to alcohol has the potential to be just as damaging as ignoring them or rebelling against them altogether. This is what happened to Sharaya and me in Kansas City, and it's what happened to me in that bar in New York.

Looking back on this story, and my question about vodka, I realize I don't have more answers now than I did then. I do, however, have more constructive questions. And if I could go back in time and talk to myself at that moment in my story, I would have asked myself why I felt like drinking on that particular night, in that particular way. I would have asked where I was headed, and if this experience was getting me what I wanted. I might have made some practical suggestions about safety and responsibility, but I would have also tried to notice how bad I was hurting, and I might have reminded myself that, no matter how much I drank, it wasn't going to fix it.

And when I do that, when I zoom out of the story and think about the difference between enjoying a glass of wine at a wedding and drinking vodka that night in New York, the delineation isn't nearly about the type or quantity of what I drink as it is about uncovering the driving forces behind my decisions. It isn't nearly as much about enforcing rules as it is about helping me see what I really wanted all along, which was to live a life that meant something and lasted longer than me.

LIVING A LEGACY

Less than two hours after we fell asleep, we woke to the unwelcome sound of our alarms warning us that if we wanted to participate in the Tunnel to Towers run we'd have to catch a cab in the next thirty minutes. I sat up in bed. My whole body felt heavy and my stomach hurt. I tried to replay the events of last night in my head. I checked my phone—still blank. I stared at the running clothes I'd laid out the night before. Sharaya turned over in bed.

"Are we doing this?" I asked her.

"I think so," she said.

Then, as if the night before had never even happened, we climbed out of bed. It made me feel better, actually, to pretend like nothing had happened the night before. I'm not sure if it was the vodka, or that it was so early in the morning, or just a general sense of denial that allowed me to wake up and step into a sort of alternate reality. But in this alternate reality I was not waiting to hear from Ben, and I had not had too much to drink the night before. Instead, I was just a runner, a friend, and a traveler who was excited to participate in a celebration of the spirit of New York.

"You seem like you're in good spirits," Gus said.

"I am," I lied, and left my phone at home.

The race started at Battery Park, on the southern tip of Manhattan Island. Our cab driver didn't seem to know where he was going, so Gus had to look up the directions and dictate from the backseat, which didn't seem to make either party very happy. Sharaya and I just clutched our water bottles and waited until we pulled as close to the crowd as we could get.

Gus paid the driver and we climbed out of the car, where more than 25,000 walkers and runners were gathering to run the race. There were firefighters, Coast Guard, Marines, Air Force, EMTs— many of them in full uniform—cheerleaders, brothers, sisters, mothers, fathers, and children of people who had lost their lives in the World Trade Center buildings on September 11, 2001.

"Today, your name is Lillian Jacobs," Gus told me. "If anyone asks. That's your name, and you don't have your ID." He turned to Sharaya. "You're just you." We giggled as we each wandered to check in and grab our race numbers. We stood in line to get our registration, stood in line to go to the bathroom, stood in line to drop off our backpacks, and then gathered with the crowd at the edge of the park where the race was about to begin.

A gun sounded, and off we went, bobbing up and down with what felt like a million other people. I thought about how each ran with a story different than ours—a story of how they arrived, what mattered to them. They told it through what they were wearing, what they were carrying, or who they waved to on the sidelines who had come to cheer them on.

"This feels like the real New York," Sharaya said to me as we ran, and I nodded. I hadn't really thought about it that way, but I knew what she meant.

If you want to experience a place, you have to experience its people, more than its landmarks, or restaurants, or ice cream, or history. You have to come into contact with the stories of the people who live there. In fact, the places from our trip with the greatest memories were the places where we spent the most amount of time getting to know the people.

But I was realizing that sometimes this also meant leaving other people behind.

Is it possible to pack light with people? Is it necessary? Is there ever a time when letting people go is the right answer? Or are relationships the things we should hold on to with the most conviction? After all, everything else can be replaced, can't it?

I thought about these questions while we ran. I thought about Stephen Silar, the man this race was created to honor. He had given up his life on September 11, along with so many others. He was on his way to a golf game with his brothers, they said, when he saw the plane hit the towers. He must not have thought twice about the decision. He must have just done it—just taken the leap, and bolted out of his car—because he knew it was right thing to do. That's the way I pictured it.

He could have known he wasn't going to make it. Still, he ran through the Battery Park Tunnel toward the two buildings on the verge of collapsing, hoping he could save a few lives. But he never came back out. We ran past cheerleading squads, loud-playing bands, and men in full uniform from the Coast Guard, the Army, and the Marines.

But what made this run unique is that no one really "raced." We all ran together, from older men in full firefighter gear to young children wearing shirts that said things like "I miss my dad."

I wondered what Stephen Silar's brothers thought later when they heard the news. I wondered if he had a wife or kids. How did they feel about their brother, their husband, or their dad, giving up everything in order to save the lives of others? Were they proud of him? Did they miss him? What were their lives like now? Had they moved on without him?

Surely no one could have imagined the legacy he would leave. They couldn't have known how many people would gather to celebrate this story—not because it was more glamorous than anyone else's, or because it had a particularly happy ending. It didn't. But because we love to celebrate stories of people who take a leap, who abandon everything to sacrifice for others. Maybe this is what makes a story worth living, worth repeating. Maybe it's what makes a chance worth taking, even when it's dangerous—the opportunity to live a life that extends beyond us, that saves the lives of others.

Sometimes our legacies force us to live without people we love. Some might leave a promising career to serve the legacy of their family; others might leave parents and siblings to be a missionary in another country. Others still might put off a relationship to write a book, to play music, or start a business. But this doesn't mean they don't leave their legacy with us. It doesn't mean they never shaped us or influenced us to begin with. And in that way, the people we love stay with us forever, even when we're not with them. And when we live our legacy, we stay with them too.

EMPTY-HANDED

Our first twenty-four hours in New York City set the pace for the rest of our week there. I was trying not to think about legacies, or about Ben, and it helped to keep moving as fast as possible. We explored the city, went shopping, ate cheap food, got lost on the subway, met up with friends for coffee or lunch, got lost on the subway again, and argued about whose fault it was that we kept getting lost on the subway. We'd rush in the door to Gus's place, say hi to Frank, ride the elevator, throw down our shopping bags, change clothes, and apply our makeup on the way to Sharaya's show. At the show she'd play, people would swoon, I'd sit in the back—selling CDs and smiling. And then we'd go home, come back the next day, and do it all over again.

All along, Ben was in the back of my mind, but the very back— where I had shoved him to keep from unraveling. I hadn't heard from him in two full days.

I didn't post on the blog the entire week. Not because I didn't have anything to say, but because there simply wasn't time, and I didn't want to slow down. *Live now, write later,* I kept telling myself as we rode the subway from one location to another, or ducked into some tiny cafe for coffee. I would make notes in my tiny Moleskine journal about what I wanted to write later, when things slowed down and got boring again. Moving fast was also a convenient way to keep my feelings at bay.

"Are you okay?" Sharaya asked as we drove to her last show in the city.

"I'm fine," I said. "Why?"

I wish she would have left it alone. I wish she would have let me live in my place of denial a little bit longer, and even come there to live with me. Maybe I could have warded off the pain that was coming. I wasn't ready to face it. But just hearing her ask me brought the weight of the situation to the surface. And even though I knew it was impossible, part of me wondered if her words did more than that. Because just then, as we pulled up to the venue, my phone rang.

It was Ben.

"I'll meet you inside," I said, holding my phone, looking down at it. Sharaya nodded her head and took her guitar. I sat in the driver's seat.

It was in the quiet of the Subaru that Ben told me he couldn't do it anymore. He gave an explanation, most of which I couldn't hear. It wasn't because there was too much noise outside—it was remarkably quiet in my little cave of personal belongings and keepsakes—but because I was having a hard time hearing over the noise of thoughts in my head. "You're just so far away," he told me. "I can hardly keep up with you. I thought I was going to be able to wait, but this just feels harder than I expected."

Harder than you expected? I wanted to say. No matter how hard I tried, I couldn't feel sympathy for him. It just didn't make any sense. We were already halfway done with our trip. In less than two months I would be in Mexico with him. We had already booked the tickets. And besides, he was the one sitting at home in a nice little apartment with all of his stuff. Harder than he expected? What about me? What about how hard this was for me? This change of attitude from him was all so sudden.

The line was silent, and I wondered if he was waiting for me to say something.

"Every day you're in a new place," he said, "and I never know who you're staying with or where you're going next. I just don't know what I would do if something happened to you. It's not supposed to feel like this. I don't want to end this, but I don't know. Maybe we can try again when you get home." He paused again.

"When I get home?" I asked.

"Yeah, you know. When you can focus more."

I couldn't believe what I was hearing. I couldn't believe he was putting me in this position. What did he expect me to do? He told me he *understood* what I was doing, and that he was supportive of me. In fact, this is what attracted him to me in the first place, wasn't it? He told me I was worth the wait, and that I shouldn't stop doing what I was doing because I was changing people. That's what he had said, wasn't it? Now he was asking me to choose? There had to be more he wasn't telling me.

But I worried the "more" was that there was someone else, or that something he had seen in me made him decide he didn't want me anymore, and I wasn't prepared to hear an answer like that. So I didn't ask.

I told him okay, that I understood, even though I didn't. Then I told him I had to go because we had a show. He asked me if I had anything else to say, and I said no. Of course, I did have other things to say, but I couldn't think. I couldn't pull them up from the depths of me and shape them into words yet. Instead, they just sat there, like rocks in my gut. I hung up. I took the suitcase of merchandise, locked the doors of our car, and walked down the street a few doors until I arrived at our venue.

I introduced myself to the bouncer, just like I did in every other city, at every other show. "I'm on the list," I told him, and asked him to direct me to the stage. I marched up the flight of stairs, just like he showed me. I unloaded the suitcase and set up the merchandise table, just like always. I listened to sound check, each of the artists one after the other, and, just like normal, thought Sharaya sounded the best. She stepped off the stage and I told her, even as she worried everyone was going to boo her off stage. She smiled, and so did I. We had this whole system down.

"Are you sure you're okay, Al?" she asked me.

"I'm fine."

That night as we drove back to Gus's apartment, I let the noise of the city press into every crack of my being. I focused on the whizzing of cars, the screeching of sirens, the yells of thick accents, and whistles across the street. I listened to the gentle swish of cash as Sharaya counted her bills in the seat next to me. The cab driver asked us where we were headed, and Sharaya asked if I wanted dinner, and I heard the inflection of their voices more than I even did their words. There was so much noise.

It wasn't until the next day, as we sped out of the city, that everything would slowly sink in—what had happened, the gravity of what I had lost. It wasn't until we left the noise of the city that I would start to see how everything was falling apart, how if I never would have left home, none of this ever would have happened. I didn't tell Sharaya what had happened with Ben, but she knew—the way you know things when you know people, by watching their face and their body language. You can almost feel what they're feeling. So she tried to give me space. She let me be quiet.

It wasn't until we arrived at Sharaya's next show—in Connecticut—and I began to set up the merchandise table, perform the sound check, and go through the motions we had repeated a hundred times that I began to see how changed I really was.

I couldn't do it. I couldn't convince people to buy Sharaya's CD. "She's just a real estate agent!" I wanted to scream to the hundred college students who had shown up to hear her play and sing. "We're both big fakers!"

Nothing made sense anymore. How could I keep blogging about "packing light" and how wonderful it was? It wasn't wonderful. It was a big crock. Letting go doesn't get you what you want. It doesn't get you anything. It leaves you empty-handed.

I was sure I had messed up along the way. I had missed the signs. If I had been more responsible, or if I had thought through my options, I would have seen this coming. I could have predicted it and prevented it. I could have saved myself all this unnecessary pain. This was it. This was my fate. I always ruined everything. I was going to be alone forever.

BLAMING GOD

I blamed God for this mess. We had made a deal, after all. I would go on this trip, He would make sure I wasn't alone. I had held up my end of the deal. What about Him? In the evenings, before I went to bed when I would have talked to Ben, I talked to God instead. I cursed Him and yelled at Him—sometimes in my head, sometimes out loud as I wandered through a strange neigh-borhood. In the mornings, an hour or two before Sharaya woke up, when I used to get my best writing done, I quit. I wasn't going to write another word. Did God think I was just going to keep writ-ing? I thought this was our deal. I thought God had promised me I wouldn't be alone—or had He? This wasn't turning out at all like I thought.

This is why I couldn't be a "Christian writer," I told myself. There was no way to write about this circumstance in a way that would be both true, and also "Christian." No matter how many Christian words I put to this, it didn't change anything. I couldn't tell everyone that no matter what happened, "God was in control." I wasn't sure He was in control. And even if He was, I was really upset about it. Why would God do this to me? I was angry, and I hated Him, and I hated myself.

The weird part was that in all these emotions, I was never quite sure where they would land. I would tell God He was a liar, and that I never wanted to talk to Him again. Then, not a minute later, I would feel all the hatred I had just pushed into the universe come rushing back at me, like a racquetball that had just struck a wall and now bounced back to smack me in the face.

I know now that it wasn't God doing this to me, but it felt like it at the time. It felt like an accusation, like a judgment of my charac-ter. *You'll never have a successful relationship,* I kept hearing. *You're doing it wrong.*

So often we make God our enemy when it's really our own shame dragging us down.

It would fluctuate like this for weeks, while Sharaya and I drove and drove, while yellow lines and green road signs went flashing by. I would get mad at God, then mad at myself. I tried to figure out how I had missed it. What had I done wrong? What had I forgotten to give up? Once again, I felt like the "rich ruler," coming to Jesus and saying, "What more do you want me to do? This time I've seriously done *everything*!"

I cried most days, although I tried to keep it from Sharaya, and from God. I wanted to be happy and have fun with Sharaya. I knew she wanted that too, and part of me felt like I was ruining it for her. That made my sadness even worse, and I sank deeper and deeper, trying to hide the depth of my grief. Trying to keep your tears from someone who lives in a car with you isn't that much different than trying to keep your tears from God, because the outcome is the same: It doesn't really work. After a while, there's a sort of mutual understanding that you're lying.

9

losing your way

"Do not pray for easy lives. Pray to be stronger men. Do not pray
for tasks equal to your powers. Pray for powers equal to your tasks.
Then the doing of your work shall be no miracle,
but you shall be the miracle."

PHILLIPS BROOKS

I WAS "FINE" ALL the way from Connecticut to Pennsylvania,
where Sharaya played two shows and we spent an aggravating
two hours driving around looking for postcards. Then we drove
to Washington, DC. A lawyer in the area, who had been following
our blog, invited us to stay with his family for a week in Virginia,
if we wanted, while we explored the area. We agreed and so found
ourselves doing much of our sightseeing from the convenient location of his home, just a short commute outside of the city.

"Which of these things do you most want to see?" Sharaya
asked me, leafing through one of the brochures our host left lying
on our bed.

"I don't care."

"The Washington Monument, obviously," she said. "And the Lincoln Memorial, and the Vietnam Memorial. These are all in the same vicinity, I think. We can probably just drive into the city and park and walk to them."

"Hmm," I said, sitting on the bed with my computer.

"You know, Maggie told me she has some friends here we should meet," Sharaya continued. "Would you be up for doing dinner with them?"

"Sure."

I had been running on autopilot for a while now. I found myself responding to Sharaya's plans mindlessly, rather than honestly. I wasn't happy, but I didn't want her to know I wasn't happy, and it was easier to pretend if I stayed disconnected from everything. Besides, if I was honest she wouldn't like what I had to say. It didn't have anything to do with monuments. The sense of adventuring we once shared together was now buried somewhere deep underneath the depression I was feeling. Through the lens of my despair, the entire world looked dark. And I was afraid if I opened my mouth, all of the venom I was feeling on the inside would come spewing out.

I thought I was making it better by keeping it to myself. I thought I was saving her from carrying the heavy weight of my baggage. But even unspoken baggage is heavy. There is no way to save people from it, to save ourselves from it. Keeping it quiet just makes it heavier.

I wanted to talk to someone. I wanted someone to understand, but the one person I wanted to call I couldn't call, and this inescapable fact made me angry. The angrier I became the more lonely I felt. Then I was so lonely I wanted to evaporate into thin air. The lonelier I felt, the more terrified I became of being alone forever. Fear is a self-fulfilling prophecy in this way. We're afraid so we act out of fear, and because we act out of fear, our fears tend to come true.

The truth, if Sharaya wanted to know it, was that I resented her. Some days I even hated her. It wasn't fair. She didn't do anything wrong, but she had something I didn't have—at least I thought she did. I wanted to feel free—like she did. I wanted to have control of my life—like she did. I wished I were as pretty as she was and that each time we went to play a show, it was me who opened my mouth to sing, and it was me people were still talking about when they left the building. I watched her, and I wanted to be like her. But I hated her for being someone I couldn't be. And I hated myself for not being who I wanted to be. Such is the paradox of jealousy.

The worst part of all was she had this way of convincing me to do things. Her confidence that everything was going to work out was contagious and irresistible. It's how she had convinced me to go on this trip in the first place. But now, I remembered her words about how I would "regret" it if I decided not to come, and it fueled my anger toward her. "You want to talk to me about regret?" I wanted to scream at her. "Let's talk about regret now!" I was thousands of miles from home, I had given up everything I owned, and the one thing I wanted when I went back to Portland was now gone—just like everything else. Regret was like a bad word burning in the back of my mouth, always one tipping point away from firing out.

Meanwhile, Sharaya was living like she always did, right in front of me, like life was just great and nothing could possibly go wrong. She had lost her condo, just like I had lost Ben. Why wasn't she hurting? Why wasn't she grieving the loss? I hated her for living like everything was just a grand adventure, everything was just a breeze, and at the same time I wanted it. I wanted what she had. Why did she get it and I didn't? I didn't want to feel the losses of what we had left behind, but the lightness of the load we had gained—like Sharaya did. But no matter how hard I tried to get myself there, I couldn't do it.

I had done everything asked of me, everything required, and here I was. I felt heavier now than I did before. I felt more confused. I felt more lost. I felt more alone. I wondered what would happen if I bought a ticket and went home. I wondered what would happen if I showed up on Ben's doorstep. What if I told him I was sorry?

But even as I thought it, I knew it was too late.

OUT WITH THE OLD

We watched the temperature drop below 45°F and pulled our warmest clothes out from beneath all of our backups in the backseat. While we rummaged, we discovered clothes and other things we hadn't seen in weeks—the mini French press Sharaya had bought at a thrift store in Colorado, a fabric flower Sharaya had worn in her hair at her Chicago show, sundresses we hadn't seen in months. Just when we would think we'd gotten to the bottom of it, we would find more. Flip-flops. Sunscreen. After-sun lotion. Hairspray we'd forgotten about. Shampoo we'd rejected. A box of headbands and earrings we loved, but never seemed to take the time to pull out of its hiding spot. We walked from the car to the guest room at least four times, and made a giant, heaping pile on our bed.

"Later," Sharaya said, "we have to get rid of some of this stuff."

We bundled up in coats and scarves and climbed into the car to drive into Washington, DC.

We had a plan, just like always. We would arrive around nine, park, and walk to the monuments and memorials we wanted to see; then, around five, we would head over to Maggie's place to meet her and some of her friends for dinner.

"You're not still thinking about Ben, are you?" Sharaya asked as we merged onto I-66E toward the city.

"No," I said.

"Because if you were still thinking about Ben," she continued, as if I had never answered, "I would have to advise you to stop that. He's moved on. So should you."

And for the rest of the drive I thought about what she said. Maybe she didn't mean "He's moved on" in a specific sense, but in a more general sense—as in "People move on after relationships." Neither of us had any way of knowing, for sure, if Ben had moved on. But at the same time I had this feeling—one of those pit-in-your-gut feelings you can't really understand or explain—that there was someone else.

I pictured him getting all dressed up the way he used to meet me for Sharaya's shows, and stopping to buy a bouquet of flowers. I pictured him standing, smiling, grinning that little-boy grin of his, knocking on a door. Then, I pictured the woman who opened that door—a more attractive, more responsible, less rambunctious, equally passionate but far more mature version of me. It could have just been my insecurity talking, or it could have been intuition. Sometimes it's hard to distinguish between the two.

Sharaya enjoyed seeing the sights and monuments. All I saw was this image of Ben with another woman—an image that stayed with me the entire day.

It was nearly four when we saw Sam for the first time. We were eavesdropping on a group tour at the Lincoln Memorial. We listened to a tour guide explain the Emancipation Proclamation and the ratification of the 13th Amendment to a group of half-attentive college students. She was holding a clipboard, and while I tried to focus my attention on her presentation, Sharaya spotted Sam in the distance.

He was clean-shaven and clean-cut, wearing a black suit, black tie, and black shoes. And if that wasn't enough to command your attention, his broad jaw and blue eyes did the trick—the kind of eyes that caught you looking and made you feel like you had just exchanged something, something important. Sharaya looked at him. He looked at her. I watched as they both tried to get a glimpse of each other out of the corner of their eyes. A few times their gazes met at the same time but Sharaya would quickly look away, the master of acting coy.

This went on for ten minutes before I stopped paying attention. The statue of Lincoln was more interesting. Or maybe I was just tired of Sharaya getting all the attention, like she always did.

Despite my growing jealousy, I couldn't deny her strategy was impressive. Sharaya would move in just the right direction at the right time, then Sam would move, and then Sharaya would move again. Each shift was small enough that you didn't know one had anything to do with the other—until suddenly, before you could really tell what was happening, the two were standing side by side.

"We need our picture taken!" Sharaya exclaimed out loud, as the tour finished and moved on to a new location. "We can't leave the Lincoln Memorial without getting our picture taken," she continued, taking her volume down a notch this time.

She looked over one shoulder, and then the other, until her eyes landed on Sam as if she didn't know he was standing there all along. Then, with a mix of pure Sharaya-like enthusiasm and a perfectly dramatized "oh-fancy-finding-you-here" look on her face, she moved toward him.

"Would you take our picture?" she asked, holding out the camera.

"Sure," he said.

He never cracked a smile the whole time he took our photo, but he also never took his eyes off Sharaya. She and I stood still, posing, smiling, as if this were just what we looked like all the time. Then, they exchanged phone numbers. I still don't know exactly how it happened. I pretended to have a sudden intense interest in the memorial architecture.

But I know that if you had been watching from a distance, what you would have seen would be worth remembering for a while. It would have been enough to lift your spirits, even if you were feeling particularly down that day. In fact, if you were a passerby, and you didn't know what was happening, you might have thought you were stealing a scene from a romantic comedy. He was a perfect gentleman. She was a beauty queen. The picture of the two of them, standing in the cold against the skyline—it was like a valentine card. Perhaps it was this image that melted the resentment for Sharaya that had been slowly building.

Later I asked Sharaya if she could teach me all her tricks. I had never seen someone so shamelessly and beautifully orchestrate a meet-cute like that. I wanted to be secure with myself like she was. Sharaya, it seemed to me, was unfailingly confident in who she was. Obviously we all have our moments of insecurity. I helped Sharaya overcome her self-doubts every time she stepped on stage. But overall, Sharaya seemed really certain that she was special, she was unique, and that everyone would be better off if and when she shared her special self with the world. And despite the deep depression that had held me down for most of the past few days, I found myself smiling again. I wanted to be just like Sharaya when I grew up.

WISHING FOR WHAT WE DON'T HAVE

We made the hike back to our car so that we could change clothes and touch up our makeup before meeting Maggie and her friends. Right there, parked on the curb of downtown Washington, DC, we brushed our teeth using our Nalgene bottles and turned our heads upside down, spraying the roots with dry shampoo until our heads didn't feel greasy anymore. This was just another day packing light. We did our makeup in the rearview mirror and chose new outfits from what was hanging in the backseat. We changed by ducking beneath the windows, putting shirts over the top of other shirts, and then, by an act of skilled acrobatics, removing the original shirt underneath. We draped blankets over our bare legs while we changed our jeans or leggings. Meanwhile, people walked by and stared, but we weren't worried about it. We had a whole system worked out.

At dinner with Maggie and her friends we sat around the table and shared stories about our trip. They listened intently and asked questions. They offered seconds, and thirds, and then dessert, until we were so full we could hardly move. It always amazed me how generous people were to us—especially when we were perfect strangers.

They reminded me of our friends back home in Portland, and I started wondering, again, why we had left. What was the point of all of this, again? We had a great group of friends back home. We had lives that made sense, and that were going somewhere, and here we were—out in the middle of nowhere—just wandering. Weren't we just wandering now? What were we actually accomplishing? At home, we had the kind of thing people want everywhere. Why did we leave it behind?

The group asked Sharaya to play for them and she agreed, reluctantly. So reluctantly, in fact, that even when she had her guitar out and on her lap at the table I was still doing lots of convincing. "They're going to love it!" I told her, just like I did at every show "You're always this nervous, and people always love you." She looked at me knowingly, but I could tell she wasn't thrilled. Each time she protested, I had an answer. By now, this was practically a script we followed. And, true to the script, she couldn't resist. She finally broke down and played a song she had just written called "Three Feet from Gold."

"This is a song about how you have to push through the hard things to get to the good stuff," she explained before she started playing.

But even though I had succeeded in convincing Sharaya, I wasn't able to convince myself of the point of all this. While she played, I couldn't pay attention.

I felt bitterness sink in deep, not just toward Sharaya, but toward each of the people sitting around the table. I felt jealous of all of them—for the lives they were living, the lives that weren't in a suitcase, the jobs that seemed more exciting and more productive than mine. I was jealous of the safety represented around this table, the kind of friendship that thrives when you live across the street from a person, when you see them every day and can call them up and grab dinner at a moment's notice. I was jealous of the pace of their lives and how predictable they were—waking up at the same time every morning, going to bed at the same time every night. I was jealous of their closets and their dressers, and the paychecks that would inevitably come each month. I was jealous of the bags of groceries in the kitchen and the fact that they could shop like that at all, not only because they had the money, but because they had a refrigerator and a pantry to keep things in.

And as Sharaya played, I felt myself fade into the background. It wasn't because she was important and I wasn't, or she was beautiful and I wasn't, or because she had a talent and I didn't, but because I believed that was the case. I believed everyone in the room had something I didn't have.

I wish I could have seen then the way I see now. It would have made things so much easier. I wish I could have known my internal world was telling me lies about my external world and what was happening in it. I wish I could have grabbed myself by the shoulders, shaken myself, and said, "No one has anything you don't have! You have everything you need. You have as much control over your life as anyone! If you feel depressed, do something about it. If you feel stuck, flail around for a while until you get unstuck. If you feel trapped, kick down the doors that are keeping you in. Make messes. Make mistakes. Just make a decision, for heaven's sake! Quit waiting for life to happen to you. Whether you're sitting in a cubicle, or on a fifty-state road trip, it's no different. The control over your life you long for, it isn't elusive. You already have it."

It's a very Christian idea to think that God has everything under control and we don't have to worry about it. It sounds really nice, but I sometimes wonder if we have misunderstood its meaning. I wonder if sometimes we take this as an excuse to do nothing.

I think about how it was the "rich young ruler" who came to Jesus, and not the other way around. It's he who acknowledged his own need ("What do I have to do to get eternal life?") and he who, when Jesus gives him the answer, responds by walking the other direction. Jesus doesn't even go running after him, which I've always found interesting. Doesn't Jesus love him? Doesn't He want him to experience the kingdom of heaven? I think He does. But I think He gives us more control than we like to admit. He leaves the final choice up to us.

It's not just inaccurate to believe we have no control—it's dangerous too. After a while you start to believe that nothing you do matters, that nothing you do will change your circumstances. If you get stuck in this place, you end up sitting around waiting on God to do something you could have done for yourself all along.

If we believe God is a dictator, barking orders down from above, after a while we start to resent Him. That's where I was. No matter how "obedient" I was to His orders, things didn't turn out the way I had planned. I've done this so many times in my life. I've turned what was always meant to be a relationship into an obedience-reward system, in which I was being obedient just to get the prize at the end. If we're being obedient to get a reward from Jesus, we'll never get it. We've missed the point. I wonder if that is what happened with the "rich young ruler." I wonder if he was worried he'd give up all of his stuff and wouldn't get rewarded.

I wish I could have known then what I know now—we already have the reward. It's days that are full and alive and hearts that are content and at rest in Him. All we have to do is let go of all our things so we can grab on to it.

It's lonely to claim no control over your life, to stand on the sidelines of a party. Trust me, I know from experience. Sure, it's safer there. No one can watch you try something new and fail. But no one can cheer you along, either. You start to feel sort of invisible, like no matter how many parties you attend, it won't matter. You still won't have any friends.

Then you start to wonder, what's the point? God's going to have His way in the end anyway, isn't He? That's what I did. And without realizing it, I set myself up to do something I would have never otherwise done.

THE ONLY WAY OUT

When we got into the car at the end of the evening, Sharaya showed me her phone. Sam had texted: "What are you girls doing tonight? Would you like to meet up for dinner?"

I shrugged. "Why not?"

And before I knew what was happening, we were on our way to Georgetown where we would meet Sam and his friend Will at a sports bar, and spend the night on what would appear to be—and what probably was—a date. They were Army Rangers, in town for a conference, and planning to stay the next few days. They were staying at a nearby hotel. They wondered, of course, what brought us to Washington, and we told them. It was the same back-and-forth explanation we gave to most people when they asked, and by now we had it down to a perfect two-part act: Sharaya first, then me, then Sharaya again, explaining what had possessed us to quit our jobs and take a six-month road trip.

I loved how amazed people always looked when we told them.

Sharaya flirted, and I marveled at her ability to be cute and coy and intellectual and engaging all at the same time.

Two hours passed effortlessly, and before I knew it we were on our third round of drinks. It was hard to believe, even when I looked at the clock, that only a few hours ago we had been at Maggie's house with all of her friends and I was feeling so disconnected. Now, we were in a totally different part of town, with a completely different group of people, acting like different people ourselves. It didn't even feel real, if I'm totally honest. "Real" would have been going back to the lawyer's house, lying awake for hours while I replayed my list of what went wrong. "Real" would have been talking to someone about how sad I was, how confused I had become, about how nothing made sense anymore. "Real" would have been calling Ben, hanging up, and then calling him again. That was the reality I had been living all by myself—a reality I wasn't exactly interested in being a part of anymore.

I looked at my phone. No new messages.

Sharaya liked Sam, and I liked Will too. Not the same way I liked Ben. I thought about the tiny hole-in-the-wall taco shop back in Portland, the starting line of what Ben and I had built together. The smells, the sounds, even the blue and white shirt he was wearing—every detail of that night was sealed in my memory with impossible accuracy. I thought about our first conversation, how easy it was, how he asked all the right questions.

Talking with Will wasn't like that. It wasn't as deep or affirming. But it wasn't bad, either. It was okay. It felt nice.

Perhaps that's why, when Sam and Will asked if we wanted to go back to their hotel with them for the night, we agreed. Their arguments were sound: it was forty-five minutes back to the lawyer's house, and it was already midnight, and we had both had a couple of drinks. I wasn't going to sleep with him; I just wanted to know I wasn't alone. It wasn't because I didn't believe in God anymore, or because I wanted to rebel against where He had called me. It was because I believed the very painful lie that my actions did not matter, that no matter what, God was going to do what He wanted.

So when we walked to the hotel room and Will reached for my hand, I let him hold it. He smiled at me, and I smiled back. Then he wrapped his arm around my shoulder and I moved in close to him. It was chilly outside, and the heat of his body kept me warm. We walked like this together and watched Sam and Sharaya walk the same way in front of us.

When we got to the hotel room, Will and I stayed up playing cards while Sam and Sharaya went for a walk. The whole thing, even then, felt like a charade. I barely knew him, yet we pretended to be so comfortable together. We played gin rummy on the hotel bed, laughing and talking, until my eyes felt heavy, and I laid my head on the pillow and fell asleep.

I woke up the next morning slowly, the way you do in a strange location after a short night of sleep. I was in a strange hotel bed with a guy I didn't even know. And the reality of what had occurred crept back in—slowly at first, until the small trickle of remembrance burst forth as a rushing river. The pain I had pushed off came flooding back. The gravity of what I had done weighed thick and heavy on me.

I had slept in my clothes. We hadn't even kissed. In fact, I'd gotten exactly what I'd wanted out of the situation. I wanted to know that I wasn't alone, that I didn't have to sleep alone or wake up alone. I wanted to know that I was pretty, that someone liked me.

But even though I had gotten all the things I wanted, I felt worse than I had the night before. Isn't this the irony of getting exactly what we think we want? Our desperate attempts to meet a need often deplete us even more. This is because we often try to silence a need by numbing it, or putting it off until later, which only makes it worse. Our coping mechanisms get bigger and more destructive, and we end up with more pain than we ever had in the first place.

Numbing pain will only make it worse. The only way out is through.

The alarm went off, and I rolled over to look at the clock. And there it was: a message on my phone from Ben. "Sorry I've been out of touch," it said. "Can you talk?"

As we drove back to the lawyer's house that morning, neither one of us said much of anything. When we got there, Sharaya slept and I tried to, but I couldn't get my heart rate to slow down. I walked out to the car and got in the driver's seat, a place I rarely sat since Sharaya drove most of the time. I put the key in the ignition. I wanted to go somewhere. I wanted to get out of this stupid driveway in this stupid city, but I couldn't think of anywhere to go.

I turned on the radio, switched the station several times, then turned it off. I climbed out of the car and swung the back door open. There were shirts and sweatshirts, shoved and wrinkled, fallen off hangers on the backseat. There were crumbs, used pieces of plastic silverware that had somehow missed our cleaning sweeps. I gathered up as much as would fit in my arms, a heaping pile I could barely see over, and marched back inside.

I marched right past the living room, where Sharaya was napping on the couch, and into the bedroom, where we had left our other pile the night before. I moved the box our host had left us to the middle of the room and started shoving things in it. *There* and *there* I wanted to say every time I threw another item in the box.

"I don't even want this anymore!" I said to myself as I threw in the top I had worn more than a dozen times on the trip. "These stupid things . . ." I tossed in my favorite pair of shoes. "I hate this!"

I said about each piece of clothing as I ripped them off hangers and threw them into the box. I didn't care if I never saw any of them again. And when all was said and done, a box nearly half my height was filled with things that, on any other occasion, I would have been sad to see go.

There, are You happy now? I screamed at God in my head, and flopped down on the bed sobbing until I, too, fell asleep.

DECISIONS, DECISIONS

I called Ben back, but he didn't answer. Then he called me, but I missed it because we were at a show in North Carolina and I was busy shooting video for the blog, setting up the merchandise table, making sure Sharaya had a bottle of water. I called him back later, but missed him again. We passed text messages back and forth. He was busy. I was busy. I was starting to think we weren't ever going to talk. Then, just after we crossed the border into South Carolina, the phone rang, and it was him.

"Can we pull over?" I asked as we drove along the coast. "I need some space to talk."

Sharaya pulled off US-17 and I stepped out of the car into the sand. I could feel it come up over the top of my flip-flops and tickle my toes. I had to speak louder than normal over the roar of the waves.

"How have you been?" I asked.

"I was going to ask you the same thing," he said.

"I've been okay."

"Me too."

The conversation was slow and awkward like it had never been before. I walked toward the water, putting one foot in front of the other, each step labored the way it is when you walk through sand. I got as close as I could to the water where the ground was still dry, and sat down.

"What's new with you?" he asked.

What was new? All kinds of things. A thousand things had happened since we had last talked, and I'd been keeping a mental list of things I had wanted to share with him. He was my closest friend, the person I wanted to start and end every day with. But now, everything I had wanted to say evaporated into thin air. All I could think about was me waking up next to Will, with a message from Ben waiting for me on my phone on the nightstand. What a slap in the face to what we had shared together.

"I'm in South Carolina now," I said.

"Wow, making progress."

"Yeah, can you hear the waves?"

The line fell silent again, and I started drawing lines with my fingers in the sand.

"What are we going to do about the tickets to Mexico?" I asked. I hadn't wanted to ask, because I wasn't really sure I wanted to know the answer. But I also needed to know, and somehow I got the impression this was going to be my last chance.

The trip was only seven weeks away. The tickets had been booked since Michigan. We had made it so far since then. And to me, his answer wasn't just about a trip to Mexico. It was a statement about where he stood with me—if he was still waiting, even though he said he wasn't. It was a statement about my future, about the future of our relationship.

"Ally," he began.

"It's okay," I said. "You don't have to say anything else."

Yes, I wanted to hear his answer, and to know all the things it represented for us. But also, I didn't. Wanting something was too risky, too dangerous, especially when I wasn't sure he wanted me back. Later, I would see pictures on Facebook that confirmed my fears that Ben had met someone else. She was, in fact, very beautiful, and she had taken my place on the trip to Mexico with his family. This realization would turn into a slow unraveling for me, a clearing up of all the confusion, a filling in the places that are so often left blank. But for now, on that beach, I was still stuck in the fog of what I didn't know. All I could do was fear and guess.

I held my phone to my ear with one hand, and put the palm of the other to my forehead. Waves crashed and I sat still in the sand.

"I loved you, Ally. I really did."

Loved. Past tense.

"I loved you too, Ben."

I hung up the phone and stood, brushing the sand off my back. I wandered back to the car with the overwhelming realization that small decisions change everything.

I don't know exactly where I started to go wrong with Ben and, who knows, maybe I didn't go wrong at all. Maybe this is the way it was "meant" to be all along. But I do know that staying with Will in the hotel room that night was the wrong decision.

It did not ruin my whole life, or even my whole trip for that matter. God is too gracious for that. But it did change my direction. It changed me. Our experiences have a way of doing this. This is why our choices matter.

I can see now, in retrospect, what I was trying to do. I had a very real need, and I was scared of what would happen if I didn't meet it. But we don't always go about filling our needs in the right way. Sometimes our attempts to fill our own emptiness are shallow and flimsy, and, in the end, don't really work. These self-made attempts will never be as deep and satisfying as if we let the only One who can reach down to the bottom of those deep, dark, scary places fill them up. This is where we find the living water, the deep, abiding presence of God, the missing puzzle piece we've been looking for all along.

Yet even though we can't meet these needs by ourself, our decisions do matter.

Some people argue that God has total control of our lives, that whatever we decide to do, it won't really matter. He'll have His way. Others want to argue that it's all up to us. Honestly, I'm tired of arguing about it. I want to live like my decisions matter—not in the sense that I can make one wrong decision and ruin everything, but in the sense that life is full of decisions and that our decisions are meaningful.

If life is a math equation, and our decisions one by one add themselves up, I want to consider what the sum of my decisions will be. When things don't add up the way I hoped they would, I don't want to blame it on God or wait for Him to fix it. I want to think about what I can do. I want to know that my choices matter.

I have grace for myself for my mistake, and I know God has grace too. But I'd be wrong to move on without saying that I'm sad about what I did. It didn't fix my loneliness like I thought it would. In fact, it made it worse.

MOVING ON

We drove south toward Sharaya's shows in Charlotte and Savannah, and as the scenery shifted and the weather warmed, my heart softened. I felt vulnerable, but not so angry anymore. I picked up a copy of Pat Conroy's *Prince of Tides* from one of our generous hosts, and I felt like the book sang the landscape to me while we drove. It's a story of grief and loss, deep love and divorce that unfolds in the swamplands of South Carolina. And just as Conroy would describe a channel or a sandbar or an old colonial home standing proud and tall, we would drive by one. He would write about the pungent smell of shrimp, and immediately I would smell it. Every now and then I would look up and out the window, and think *"Exactly,"* and then put my head back down into my book.

Sharaya and Sam stayed in touch, text messaging and smiling all the way through the marshes, past signs for boiled peanuts and Piggly Wiggly grocery stores.

Watching them, of course, made me miss Ben. But my melancholy melted in the face of thick Southern accents, charm as sweet as their sweet tea, and delicious hospitality. I loved the way men would open doors for women, and women would dress up just to go get groceries. I loved being warm—wearing short sleeves and shorts and cowboy boots every day and not feeling the slightest bit out of place.

Sometimes at night, when I thought I was finally starting to find some peace, I would lie awake and wonder what she looked like—the girl Ben had chosen instead of me. I couldn't decide if I was just being paranoid there was another girl, or if I was positively sure there was someone else. She was pretty, I imagined. She was sweet. And I bet she never let some adventure get in the way of loving him.

Strangely, it was this painful break that finally gave me the space and time to write. My phone was now silent. Ideas had all kinds of room to grow. The words came more frequently and freely as I blogged; they were less superficial and more meaningful. They did a better job of bringing our experience to life. Our audience grew.

LOVE IS A RISK

We drove from Charleston to Savannah, where Sharaya's friend Lindsey welcomed us into her beautiful Southern home. It was exactly the kind of home you expect to see in the South—white and colonial. And it was in exactly the kind of neighborhood that feels safe and reassuring—with quiet streets where kids can ride their bikes and parents can trust them to go to the end of the block and back without supervision. This is the kind of neighborhood where you want your kids to grow up.

There was fresh bread baking in the oven when we walked in, and our host's living room was decorated elegantly with dark wood furniture. You could still see the vacuum lines in the living room carpet. Lindsey greeted us at the door in her apron, wiping flour from her hands before giving us both big, gracious hugs.

She invited us into the house and showed us where we would be staying. There was a *Norton Anthology of English Literature,* a Bible, and a book of Philip Larkin poems sitting on the coffee table. There were two other books, propped open so that I couldn't see the titles, right next to Lindsey's computer.

"Don't mind my mess," she said with a smile. "I'm getting my master's in literature. This is how I keep myself busy while my husband is deployed."

I could already tell I was going to like her.

She had separate rooms prepared for us upstairs. Each of our rooms had a basket with bottles of water, a magazine, hand towels, and a card welcoming us to her home. I smiled as I read her handwriting across the top: "Guest Information Card." The card had numbered instructions below, like "Extra towels can be found in the closet in the hallway," and "If you leave here hungry, it's your fault."

Lindsey took us to see the city of Savannah, where we strolled down River Street and wandered in and out of shops. Every once in a while she would put on her best tour guide voice and say, "If you'll notice here to the left, there's a giant ship floating down the river, but on the right, there's a chocolate store. Now, let's talk about which one is more exciting." Despite her Martha Stewart exterior, Lindsey had a little spunk to her that kept Sharaya and me laughing and smiling the whole afternoon.

I asked her to tell me about her husband's job in the military, and what it was like for him to be deployed. I admitted how little I knew about military life, and that, until recently, I hadn't really known anyone in the military. She told me how she and her husband had met, and that shortly after he had enlisted as an officer. Now he was stationed in Savannah. Lindsey had moved her entire life from Oregon to Georgia, and now that her husband was deployed, she didn't even have him. It was awful, she said, and never got easier.

"The first thing I did when he left this time was spend $400 at Pottery Barn," she told me. "I knew he was going to be so mad when he saw the charge on the credit card, but I didn't care at the time. I was just trying to keep myself busy."

"You're packing light too," I said. "It looks really different than it does for us, but you are. You gave up everything. You have to keep doing it every day."

"Yeah, I guess that's true."

We nodded together, and took bites of the chocolate we had stopped to buy. Sharaya told Lindsey about Sam, how'd they'd met in Washington, and how they'd stayed in contact since then. She told Lindsey that he was an Army Ranger, and the two of them talked about what it was like to be with a man in the military.

"He wants to come to Savannah while we're here," Sharaya said. "He's only a couple of hours away."

"To take you on a date?" I asked.

Sharaya smiled.

"What a gentleman!" Lindsey and I exchanged looks.

For the next few hours we wandered in and out of shops and restaurants. Sharaya bought a new top, charging it to her credit card. We walked into a restaurant, just to see what it looked like on the inside, and she asked to see a menu. I was pretty sure she was scouting a restaurant for her date with Sam—a subtle giveaway for her excitement.

At one point she caught her reflection in a mirror, and paused for a second to smooth a flyaway strand of hair and fix her wayward lip gloss. If you hadn't been watching closely, you might have missed it. If you didn't know her, you might have thought it was meaningless. But I knew her, and I was pretty sure I knew what it meant. I could feel the anticipation building. I was happy for her but, of course, I was also worried. Love is always a risk.

HOW ARE YOU SUPPOSED TO KNOW?

Sharaya's date drove four hours to come take her out on a Friday night, and when he arrived at the front door, Lindsey and I were on the couch reading poetry and writing blog posts. Sharaya was upstairs getting ready. There was a cheesecake baking in the oven so the house smelled like vanilla and heaven.

The doorbell rang and Lindsey rose from her seat.

"Hello," I could hear Lindsey's short and simple greeting at the front door, and Sam's low voice echoing into the hallway. I stood and walked toward the front door, and there he was—standing with his black pants and his blue shirt tucked in, with a belt and shiny shoes. "Hey, Sam," I said, giving him a stiff wave. I tried to smile.

He nodded. Lindsey gestured for him to sit on the wooden bench at the front door.

"I have a standing rule about strange men in the house while my husband is deployed," Lindsey said. "You understand." And with that, she turned and walked out of the room. "Have to check on the cheesecake!" she called behind her, and then to Sharaya, "Sam is here!"

The two of us stood there in the hallway, awkwardly trying not to look at each other. I wasn't sure if I should stick my hand out for a handshake, or just lean against the wall like I was doing.

I wanted to tell Sam that we weren't the type of girls who go with guys back to their hotel rooms. We were respectable women. I wanted him to have Sharaya home by midnight, and to treat her like a gentleman would. But every time I opened my mouth to speak, I worried it would come out sounding too parental, too embarrassing, so instead I just turned on my heels and said, "I'm going to check on Sharaya."

Upstairs, Sharaya was putting the finishing touches on her makeup. She was wearing a new top and her blonde hair was sprayed in perfect position. I thought about telling her to be careful. I thought about warning her to take it slow and not to set herself up for disappointment. After all, Sam lived across the country, and she barely knew him. We didn't know anything about his family, or his church, or his friends. The meeting had been so random, and so—well, unconventional with the monument and the hotel room. It could either make for a really good story, or a really dangerous one.

But even as all of this brewed, I watched her smile and take one last look in the mirror. "How do I look?" she asked.

"Beautiful," I said.

So Lindsey and I sent Sharaya and Sam off on their date like a couple of worried parents, and then we preoccupied ourselves otherwise for the night. We read and talked about poetry, and she taught me all the tricks about getting a cheesecake out of the springform pan—the most notable of which meant we had to wait until tomorrow to eat it.

"You have to let it cool for at least twelve hours," she said. "Plus, you need to get it out of the oven before it looks done. That's the secret." She stood at the kitchen counter, pointing to her perfect cheesecake, and I stood next to her, rinsing pots and pans. I stopped for a minute and turned toward her.

"Do you think Sam and Sharaya will work out?" I asked.

She paused before answering. "There's no way to know."

I nodded.

"Look, I think you're a lot like me," she said. "And if that's true, I know you want to know the answers to things. But there are some things in life—more things than not, probably," she paused. "There's just no way to know." She shook her head. "There's just no way to know."

I wanted to tell her about Ben, about everything that had been going on in my head, about wondering if I had done something wrong, if I had messed it up, if maybe I should abandon everything and go home. I wanted to ask her opinion. But instead I just picked up glasses from the dishwasher and slowly loaded them into the cupboard. They made gentle clinks as I set them down.

"If anyone tells you they have the answers, Ally, they're lying. There are no guarantees. You just have to take the information you have, and make the best decisions you know how. Then, if it doesn't work the way you thought it would, you have to admit your mistake and get up and try again. I've been a Christian my whole life, and I love Christians. But Christians love to make life sound so much easier than it is. Life isn't black and white. Life doesn't come with a rule book. We have boundaries and guidelines, and we have a conscience. We even have the Spirit of God living in us, but we don't have any guarantees. If someone sells you a guarantee, they're ripping you off."

It tortured me, the idea of not knowing. I could tell it sort of tortured Lindsey too, but somehow she seemed like she had come to terms with it. I wanted that too—the quiet resolve she had; the sureness of spirit. Funny how she had stopped trying to figure out the meaning to everything, and meaning had just come to her. Meanwhile, I was trying to wrestle meaning to the ground, and it was torturing me.

10

open hands

"He who has God and has many things has nothing
more than he who has God alone."
C. S. LEWIS

WE LEFT GEORGIA AND drove south to Florida, where a friend of mine from high school was stationed at an Air Force base. She lived there with her husband, and they had agreed to host us for a few days. This time I offered to drive, and Sharaya let me.

On the drive to Florida I felt the warmth of the sun through our windshield and the warmth of the conversations with Lindsey melt away any residual jealousy and bitterness I had felt toward Sharaya for the way her romance was only beginning just as mine came to a bitter end. It was a slow process. I felt like a city coming back to life after a long winter. I still didn't have all the answers, but like Lindsey had said, I didn't need to.

Florida was warm and salty and the seafood was fresh; the minute it dropped below eighty degrees the women pulled out wool sweaters to ward off the chills. The sun itself seemed to be different in Florida. I couldn't explain it exactly, but especially in the early parts of the evening, the sky turned into a palette of blues and purples and yellows that I had never seen before. Maybe it was the reflection of those colors onto everything else, but for whatever reason the whole world seemed to glow.

"Aren't you chilly in those shorts?" a gas station attendant asked me, just after we crossed the Florida border.

"Oh no. I'm from Oregon. When it gets this warm in Portland people lie on their front porches in swimsuits drinking lemonade and spraying themselves with spray-bottle fans."

Erin took us to the Air Force base where we took kayaks into Chattahoochee Bay. We paddled ourselves out a safe distance from the shore and floated in the middle of the ocean, stinging and sticky from the salt water, watching intently for dolphins. That was our Florida thing—you know, the "thing" you really want to do when you visit a place, just to say you did it.

Florida. Dolphins. It just seemed right.

So we floated, waiting, paddles draped across our laps, leaning far back in our kayaks so as to let the UV rays do their work to bronze our pasty Oregon skin. And as we lay there, Erin turned to me and said, "So, how do you know when you're packing too light?" The gentle waves rocked my yellow boat.

"Packing too light?" I said. Erin had been following our journey and our metaphor through our blog.

"Yeah. Like, you don't want to leave your toothbrush behind. How do you decide what's your toothbrush and what's an extraneous pair of shoes? Metaphorically speaking."

There was a slow silence, and in it the question I had long been asking myself buoyed to the surface.

I don't know if it was her question or sunbathing in October, but either way, my head was spinning.

Erin didn't know about Benjamin, but that's what I was thinking about. She didn't know that, just days earlier, I had been in Georgia with Lindsey, having a conversation just like this. I hadn't thought about my relationship with Ben in terms of packing too light. Why hadn't I thought of that? But I had wondered if there were some times when you should hold on to something at all costs.

I rehearsed the metaphor in my mind. Packing light. Letting go of what holds you back. Baggage. Baggage is bad. And in my mind I kept having flashes of Sharaya and me on the road with a completely empty car, living for five months without pajamas or a toothbrush or even a change of underwear.

Are there some things in life we should never let go of? Is learning to let go as important as learning to hold on? How do we know the difference? How do we know when to do which?

After an hour in the blazing October sun, we still hadn't seen any dolphins, so we paddled back to shore, defeated. We climbed from our kayaks and pulled them out of the water and onto the soft shore. We trudged through the doughy beach, pulling our kayaks behind us to the sound of thick plastic against grainy sand. We flipped the big yellow barrels upside-down and back on their high racks. And the whole time my mind was spinning with ideas about what it meant to pack too light, about when to hang on and when to let go, and about the fact that we never did see any dolphins.

Sometimes we let go because we want to. I pictured us unloading our car onto a bed or into a parking lot and sifting through items we hadn't seen in months, items we'd forgotten we even had. We had already sent three big boxes home and, to be honest, I didn't even remember what was in them. Sometimes we let go of something, or leave it behind, because it no longer serves its purpose and it just doesn't make sense to keep it. A broken car, for example; a malfunctioning French press, or a giant cooler that takes up too much room in your backseat. This kind of packing light is liberating. There's such a feeling of accomplishment as you clear out the clutter and lighten your load. It just plain feels good.

Other times, "letting go" is totally out of our control. We lose things or they get broken or stolen. Life happens, and computer chargers or favorite sweaters or curling irons are ripped from our reluctant grasps. Sometimes when to let go is decided for us.

Then there is a time when packing light does not feel good. This is a time when packing light feels like grief, which feels very much like fear.

As I sat on the beach at sunset, warm and gratified, I realized I wasn't thinking about the answer to my question anymore. I was dragging my fingertips through the cream-colored sand, shaking my head, smiling. I was thinking about how I was on a beach in shorts in October. I was thinking about the profound demonstrations of hospitality shown to us on this trip, about how little I really understand about truly living in need, and about this old, stupid metaphor I'd heard about what happens to sand when you squeeze it. I picked up a handful and closed my fingers tightly. The sand spilled quickly from my grasp.

Open hands, I thought. That's the answer. Open hands to receive gifts that come, enjoy them while they last, and give freely when it's required. Open hands that live gracefully, with gratitude, with or without a toothbrush. And as quickly as the thought came to me it also left because I heard a voice yelling in the distance. "Dolphins!" the voice was saying. "Look!"

I brushed the sand from my back and walked down toward the waves. There they were, just beyond the wake—three or four of them, flinging their agile bodies out of the water, playfully, so that I could see.

REACHING OUT, GRABBING ON

Our last night in Florida we carved pumpkins. It was Halloween after all, and it only felt appropriate, even on a fifty-state road trip.

"How can we go to Louisiana in the least amount of time?" Sharaya asked as she dug pumpkin guts out with an orange plastic scraper.

It was not an easy task mapping out our next steps while our hands were sticky and covered in pumpkin.

We wanted to go to New Orleans, but we were running out of money, and we couldn't find a place to stay. We had exhausted all of our contacts, even staying in Florida for an extra two days, waiting to hear from one that we were pretty sure was going to pan out but never did. My friend Erin and her husband, Mike, had been generous in letting us stay, but I was starting to feel like we were overstaying our welcome. And we were both getting nervous about making it to Sharaya's shows in Arkansas, Oklahoma, and Texas.

I rinsed my orange pumpkin guts scraper in the sink, dried my hands, and pulled out my phone. I opened the Maps application and zoomed in on Florida and Louisiana. I traced my finger along the way.

"Looks like Monroe," I said. "It's right on the highway."

"Perfect," she said.

"I wonder what there is to do in Monroe, Louisiana?"

"I guess we'll see tomorrow!"

It was settled. We would leave early tomorrow morning, drive to Monroe, Louisiana, then to Little Rock, Arkansas, then on to our last six states. We'd be home before Christmas. I couldn't believe we were getting this close.

Sharaya took the pumpkins we had carved and set them artfully on the front porch, candles cheerily glowing inside. Then she went to bed. I stayed up thinking about what life was going to look like after the road trip. I felt like I was holding an Etch-A-Sketch, one I had spent hours happily doodling on only to have my big brother come and shake it up so the drawing was gone. *I guess I should get to etching again,* I thought to myself.

So I started dreaming. A lot had changed since I had started on this trip. If my life wasn't going to look how I thought it was, what did I want it to look like? Did I even want to be a writer? Did I want to write a book? Did I want to live in Portland? I had just been introduced to all of these wonderful places, and I didn't have anything tying me back to Portland, did I? I could live anywhere.

I thought about my favorite stops of the trip. Not Deadwood, but other favorites—the kind of favorite cities where I would want to live. Boulder. Boston. Chapel Hill. Ann Arbor. These places stuck out in my mind, places where people were always on a mission to learn something or try something new. I loved that you rarely saw someone without a book or a book bag or a laptop, and when you walked by people in restaurants you could catch snippets of deep, fascinating conversations.

So I started researching cities, college towns, and jobs available in each of them. I thought about being an English teacher, or maybe getting my doctorate or my MFA. In fact, why limit myself to the United States? I could go teach overseas. Teachers overseas made quite a bit of money. I researched Department of Defense schools, international schools, and what kind of certification I needed to work there. I looked in Germany, China, Argentina, Ecuador. Ending the relationship with Ben, as painful as it had been, left a whole new world of opportunities open to me.

This is another thing that makes letting go difficult. The things in our life—people, places, experiences, dreams—all rest on each other, like blocks in a building. Some are more important than others, some are less so. Some of them are integral. Some are the foundation. But move enough blocks, even the secondary ones, and everything starts to crumble.

Sometimes we build with the wrong blocks, or we put the right blocks in the wrong places, and it makes our building vulnerable.

That's what I did with Ben, and even with my book. And when it falls, it feels tragic, but it's really just a chance to pick each of the blocks up again, evaluate them, and decide. Which am I going to build with this time, and where am I going to put them?

It happens to all of us. Maybe we have our whole story resting on a certain place we want to go to school, or a city where we want to live, or the idea that we'll write a book, or get married, or have kids. What do we do when it doesn't work out? What do we do when we don't get what we thought we wanted? We can either choose to feel like it's the end of the world, or we can choose to decide it's the beginning.

By the time I looked at the clock again it was two in the morning and I was still staring into the blazing face of my computer. I pulled my hair up high on top of my head and shifted in my seat to keep my legs from falling asleep.

I thought about my conversation with Lindsey back in Savannah. "There are no guarantees," she had said. Then she had listed three things that help us find our way: we have boundaries, we have our conscience, and we have the Spirit of God living inside of us.

So I prayed. It wasn't a wordy prayer—in fact, I'm not sure it had any words at all. It was more like a deep breath, a small surrender of the heart. If I had to put words to it, they would go something like this: *Okay, God—now what?*

What happened next was so subtle I would wonder later if it really happened or if I was just making it up to make myself feel better. Either way, I felt these words rise up from inside of me, like they had been there all along: *You're not alone.*

I remembered the deal I had made with God back in Oregon, at the beginning of all this. I bartered with Him—told Him I would go on this trip but that I didn't want to be alone. I thought Ben was the answer to that prayer, and when I met Will I had tried to answer the prayer for myself, but maybe I'd had the answer to the prayer all along. Maybe I'd had the answer before I even asked. God had been with me this whole time.

I called a truce with God before we left Florida. I told Him that I wouldn't yell anymore, and that I wasn't mad, and that I wanted to keep talking. I'm pretty sure He told me it was okay that I yelled, that He was tough and could take it, and that He would be happy to talk to me anytime I wanted.

One of the hardest parts of packing light, I've learned, is that it's as much about what you take with you as it is what you leave behind. Letting go of everything isn't the answer. In fact, sometimes letting go is the easy part. But packing light isn't as simple as throwing up our hands and leaving everything up to God. It's as much about holding on as it is about letting go—and knowing the difference between the two.

It matters what you put in your suitcase.

Sometimes, the options overwhelm us. Or at least they overwhelm me. If decisions matter, if they add up to something, then I want to make decisions carefully. But things get complicated when you can pick from a dozen different colleges instead of just three. How do you know which one is right? How do you make the best choice? You could apply to hundreds of different jobs all across the country. You could date or marry one of five, or ten, or fifty different men. You could live in this city or that one. The options are limitless. How are you supposed to pick? How do you choose what to put in your suitcase? How does anyone know the right decision?

That's what I was wondering as we packed our car. I thought about it as we traveled down the interstate, listening to Fiona Apple, coffee in hand, watching ahead of us as the early morning fog began to lift.

THE BEST KIND OF JEALOUSY

We drove to Monroe, which didn't have much to offer unless you've never seen a Super Target. Other than that, there were six Bail Bonds buildings on a single block, each with gaudy signs painted in neon colors, and not much in the way of postcards, but we made do. Needless to say, we didn't stay long. There's only so long you can stay entertained by a Super Target when you don't have any money.

So we drove to Arkansas listening to our Taylor Swift CD—an album we weren't ready to admit we owned that had been an impulse purchase at a Starbucks a few states earlier. It's funny the things that will happen when you're tired, and haven't had your coffee, and someone puts something pink and shiny in front of you. Starbucks is smart like that. So is Taylor Swift.

I sat in the driver's seat and, at one point, I looked over to find Sharaya peeling open a little Laughing Cow cheese Erin had graciously packed for us and smearing it onto a rice cake with her finger. She was so focused and intent, I couldn't help but burst out laughing. Once she realized what I was laughing about she looked at me and her face lit up.

"Want one?" she asked.

"Actually, yes!"

So we listened to Taylor Swift a few more times through, and I would be lying if I said I didn't give her a few fist bumps, or sing a couple angry one-liners with her as I thought about Ben. It was just too tempting. Then Sharaya turned the music down.

"I have an idea," she said.

She had that look on her face—the road trip look, the same look she'd had at the wedding months earlier, the same one she always had when she was scheming something. I listened while she told me about how, after the trip, she was thinking of moving to Nashville. After all, she didn't have her condo back in Portland anymore, and that was really the only thing tying her there. Nashville had a great music scene, she said, and it would be the next logical step in her music career.

She explained how, when we got back, she would just sell everything that was left from her apartment and leave right away.

"I've been looking at places," she said, "and I think I can get one for pretty cheap. I think I could make it happen."

I knew that if anyone could make it happen, Sharaya could. She was the most resourceful, innovative person I knew. Still, the thought of her leaving didn't make me feel great. I would miss her if she left. And without her, it made me feel insecure about my own direction in life. She was so much more put together than I was. But if she wanted to move to Nashville, I would support her decision.

"You'll be amazing. Nashville will be lucky to have you." And I meant it.

I was proud of her, but I was jealous too, if that makes sense. But this time it wasn't a mean jealousy; it was a healthy jealousy. I think there's a difference. Mean jealousy pulls people down so they'll be on the same level with us, or pushes them down on our way up. But a healthy jealousy is sometimes just the push we need to jump for ourselves. Sometimes we need to look at someone who is doing something difficult, or dangerous, so that we know we can do it too. It's that sense of "I want what you have," that makes the risk seem worth it.

It reminded me of the waterfall jump in Costa Rica. I just had to watch a few other people do it before I was ready. We see someone else taking the risk and surviving, and we figure we want to do it too. I think this is okay, even normal. I think this is a place where jealousy is necessary, healthy even, because it inspires us to make our next move.

So I watched Sharaya take a mental jump, and then an actual one. Over the next few days, and then weeks, she began making plans for her big move to Nashville. It became the topic of conversations, and phone calls between her and Sam. They would only be a few hours apart from each other, after all, if she moved to Nashville. This was making more and more sense. A few hundred miles was far more attainable than a few thousand. This could turn into a viable long-distance relationship.

I watched all the pieces come together for Sharaya, and the jealousy, healthy jealousy, inside me grew.

EXPERIENCED TRAVELERS

Thanksgiving was days away, and my cousin was getting married in Texas. My parents, along with my sister and her husband, flew from Portland, and Sharaya and I raced from her last show in Tulsa to make it in time for the wedding. Despite our best efforts, we arrived minutes after the bride and groom had already said "I do." There was a casual reception afterward—punch and cookies, that sort of thing. We decided later this was probably a good thing, since we were wearing jeans and sweatshirts and didn't have anything to offer as a gift.

But we stepped out of the car to people who knew us, who hugged us and told us they were so glad we were safe. We shared meals that had way too many calories to count but that filled us in ways that food just can't do by itself. We played games and stayed up too late and laughed too much, if that's even possible.

Seeing my family again was like a pause button—a place to let down, to be totally ourselves for a while, before moving on.

I told my sister the whole story about Ben, and she listened. I lamented how much love hurt, and how I wasn't sure if I wanted to do it again.

"I understand," she said. "Love is on the horizon for you. I believe that."

I was glad someone did.

One night as we ate, I looked around the room at my grandma, who was getting older now, struggling to get her plate and scoot to her place at the table. I watched my aunt making sure everyone got something to eat before she did. I watched my sister sit on the floor in front of her husband, who was on the couch. They hadn't been married very long; their love was still fresh and new. He put his hands gently on her shoulders, and my parents smiled at them from across the room.

It occurred to me how growing something deep and rooted might be better than growing it wide. It made me think about how our lives start far before we're ever born, and how they go on without us when we leave. It made me think broader and more multifaceted about what it means to live a good story. My story isn't just about me.

I wasn't sure exactly what that meant, or what to do about it, but I was pretty sure it changed everything.

We left Dallas after four days, not because we were ready, but because it was time. Sharaya had two other shows to play in Texas, then one in New Mexico, then two in Arizona. Determined to find her a place to play near the Grand Canyon—mostly so we could have an excuse to go see it—I started calling resorts in the area to see if one would trade us a night's stay for a concert. It was a long shot, but we figured if I could make Sharaya sound important enough, we might be able to make it happen. I had a list in front of me of all the resorts within a twenty-mile radius.

"Yes, hello," I would say when the operator answered the phone. "I'm the agent for artist Sharaya Mikael out of Portland, Oregon, and we're about to pass through your part of town. We have a break in our tour. Would you be interested in booking a show at a reduced rate?" If the person on the other end of the line showed even the slightest bit of interest, or even if they just paused for a minute, I would add, "We would even be willing to do an exchange for food and lodging."

On about the sixth phone call, we found one who was interested.

"Let me call you back," the manager said. We waited.

And that's how Sharaya ended up playing a show at a cocktail lounge in Sedona, Arizona. Not only playing a show, in fact, but also having an open tab for as much food and drink—steak, wine, eggs Benedict for breakfast the next morning—as we wanted. Not only that, but the manager gave us two free coupons for spa treatments so we could get complimentary massages or facials. We did yoga classes every morning, since it was free for guests, and one morning while we were relaxing calmly in Child's pose, I looked over at Sharaya and said, "Why didn't we think of this before?"

She shrugged her shoulders, the best you can in Child's pose.

So we did the same thing in New Mexico.

We drove to a resort in Carlsbad, and Sharaya played to a dining room of people while they were eating. She didn't particularly like doing that, but I knew from eavesdropping on conversations that they were grateful for the entertainment. They gushed over her voice and how pretty she was. She could never hear any of that while she was playing, so I would always tell her afterward. Sometimes she would even believe me.

Somehow all the attention Sharaya was getting now didn't bother me anymore. It didn't feel like she had anything I didn't have. It didn't feel like we were competing. We were on the same team. We were doing life together—both of us were getting our hands messy and making something beautiful together. I was pretty sure this is what family did, and Sharaya was like family to me.

As we checked out of the hotel in Carlsbad, we noticed postcards sitting on the counter. Sharaya pointed to them and looked at me.

"Are these for sale?" she asked the concierge.

"Actually, they're complimentary," he said.

"Can we have fifteen of them?"

We savored those last few weeks of the trip, understanding, I think, that they would be coming to a close so soon. We tried to be a little more open, laugh more often, share music, share thoughts, share our things. Soon Sharaya would be in Nashville, and I would be back in Portland. We wouldn't be able to do this forever.

Maybe that was the reason we made a quick stop in Las Vegas. We didn't have a show booked there, but neither of us had ever been, and it was the most logical stop between Sedona and Las Angeles. Plus, we heard that some of our friends were going to be in town. We decided to stay overnight and spend the afternoon with them the next day.

A blog follower and friend had booked a room for us at a hotel, insisting that we absolutely couldn't drive through Nevada without the experience, so we checked in and immediately left to go find dinner. We wandered through the hotel casino, passed slot machines and fancy restaurants. Everything was lit up and flashing, making noises and singing. People were laughing, excited to be out on the town and dressed to the nines, but, I don't know, they just seemed very lonely to me. I wondered at one point if the girls working the casinos were issued a standard uniform that consisted of the tiniest piece of fabric you've ever seen and then a giant pair of high heels. Every single one was wearing the same thing.

"Are you girls Mormon?" one guy asked later that evening while we were at dinner. I'm assuming he was referencing our fitted jeans, long sleeved solid-color shirts, and the colorful scarves wrapped around our necks—the nicest clothes we had that were still weather-appropriate for December.

"Very funny," Sharaya said, and he turned back to his friends, laughing.

We wandered around looking for our car for a good hour and a half before we found it. One thing they don't tell you about casinos is they don't have any easily accessible exits. So we found the only exit we could find, and walked the long way around, until we finally found the lot where we had left it several hours earlier. We both climbed in and looked at each other.

"I think I'm ready to move on," Sharaya said.

"Me too."

We both smiled, and drove back to our hotel.

11

choose your path

"Don't ask yourself what this world needs. Ask yourself
what makes you come alive, and do that. Because what
this world needs are people who have come alive."
JOHN ELDREDGE

WE ARRIVED IN LA and you could feel it in the air—the winding
down. Sharaya was making plans to leave for Nashville. I was making plans to pick life back up again with Rebecca in our apartment
back in Portland. You could feel it start to happen—this collision
of the road-trip life we had been living with all of the "real world"
stuff we were going to embrace again.

Our friends Beks and Steve invited us to stay with them. Beks
and I had known each other since we were in elementary school.
We had grown up together, and I had watched her date Steve, and
fall in love, and finally get married. They assured us that if we didn't
stay with them, they would be deeply offended, so we agreed. They
set us up in their living room and bought us food from Trader Joe's
and made us feel at home from the minute we arrived.

The Christmas party in the Arts District was Beks's doing—or at least hers along with a few other friends. At first, I wasn't going to go.

"I don't have anything to wear," I whined to Sharaya earlier in the day.

"I don't care," she said. "You're coming, and you're going to have fun."

So it was with reluctance that I dressed up with Beks and Sharaya that night, borrowing a dress so that I didn't feel so out of place. And with the brownies I had made earlier that day on my lap, Sharaya and I crammed into the backseat of Beks's Mini Cooper and made our way to the party. Beks drove, and Steve sat in the front seat.

"I want to hear everything," Beks said as she drove, glancing back at us in her rearview mirror. "I've read the blog, but I want the behind-the-scenes stuff."

She had gotten home from work less than an hour before we had to leave for the party, just barely enough time for her to hug us, get dressed, and do her makeup for our evening out. So this was the first real conversation we'd had.

"What do you want to know?" I asked her.

"What do you tell people when they ask what you do, Ally?" she asked, and silence followed.

"I mean, it's pretty obvious what Sharaya does. She sings every night. But what do you say? Do you say you're a groupie? A manager? Do you tell them you're writing a book?"

Her words stung in a way only Beks could make them—just soft enough so you knew she meant well, but sharp enough that she could cut straight to the issue.

The worst part was, she knew me really well. She knew that, when people asked me what I was doing on the trip with Sharaya, I wasn't going to say that I was writing a book. I wasn't going to talk much about how I was keeping a blog, and when they asked me what I did for a living, I was going to have a near nervous breakdown because I didn't know how to answer their question. But it wasn't because I was modest. It was because I was insecure. I knew what I wanted to tell people, I just couldn't bring myself to say it out loud.

"I don't know what I do for a living," I said. "Am I a teacher? Am I a groupie? Am I a road manager? A publicist?"

"What do you want to be?" Beks asked.

"I want to be a writer, but that doesn't mean I am one. You don't get to just decide what you're going to be—do you?"

The car engine hummed while we stood still at a red light.

"Isn't that what I'm doing?" Sharaya asked.

I thought about it for a minute. My legs were scrunched behind Steve in the passenger seat, who was quiet during our discussion, and the brownies sat warm on my lap.

"What if you just started telling people that you were a writer?" Beks suggested. "What if you just did it for one night?"

"I guess so . . ." I said.

"I dare you," she continued. "At the party tonight, when people ask you what you do for a living, just start saying it. 'I'm a writer. I'm writing a book. I write for a living.'"

"I'll consider it."

"What do you have to lose? There will be people at this party who you'll never see again. They may only have a few minutes to know you. What are you going to tell them? What impression are you going to leave them with?"

I wondered if she was right.

We arrived at the party—a plain, cement-walled warehouse with "Arts District Christmas" projected with white lights on the building outside. I looked behind me. *How did they do that?* I wondered. LA was way too cool for me. I took a deep breath, brownies in hand, and walked through the front door.

We weren't the first ones there by any stretch of the imagination, but you could tell we were not-so-fashionably on time. There was a handful of beautiful women in stunning dresses—much more modest than the ones we'd seen in Vegas just a few days earlier—clustered in groups in the wide open space.

"People show up to parties hours late sometimes," Beks explained. "It's like the more important you think you are, the later you show up. But this whole thing was my idea, so I figured I should get here early enough to help."

The lights were low and the space was wide open—though with the dance music playing and strobe light spinning in the center of the room, it wouldn't be empty for long. I went straight to the kitchen to ask if I could help. And as we arranged food on the long, wooden table against the back wall, the warehouse slowly began to fill up.

I thought about my party strategy—how normally, at a party like this, I would stick to the edges and stay out of the mess. But for some reason, tonight I decided I wasn't going to do that anymore. I was going to get into the party.

"Ally, I want you to meet my friend Jess," Beks would say, and Jess and I would shake hands. Then she would explain to me who Jess was, how she knew him, what he did for a living—some interesting fact—then she would vanish.

She did this a couple of times before I met Eve. Eve worked for a nonprofit in the area as their director of marketing. She was originally from Austin but she had been living in LA for four years now. She was one of those people who make small talk easy—filling the conversation with genuine interest in what you were saying, and her wide smile.

"What do you do?" she asked. I wondered for a minute if Beks put her up to it. But even if she did, I decided to give it a try.

"I'm a writer."

"What kind of writing do you do?"

"I have experience in several areas," I said, for a moment feeling like I was reading off my resume. "I've done some copywriting, lots of academic writing, and I'm currently working on a book."

"Oh, really? What's the book about?"

"My friend Sharaya and I," I pointed to her across the room, "are just finishing a road trip across the whole country. She's a musician. I kept the blog while we were traveling, and now I'm writing a book about it. It's called *Packing Light*." I was about to pull Sharaya's card out of my purse and invite her to Sharaya's show at Hotel Cafe the next evening, but before I could, Eve said, "My company is looking to hire a writer. Do you have a resume?"

And just like that, we set up a time to meet the following morning and I told her I would bring my resume along with me. Eve thanked me and moved on to another conversation, and suddenly there I was—standing right in the middle of the bustling party, with nothing in my hands to make me appear occupied, no one to talk to, looking like an idiot—with the biggest smile on my face.

I wonder if I'm not the only one who panics when people ask that dreaded question—*what do you do?* There is so much wrapped up in it, so much that has nothing to do with a job. We worry it says something about our identity to say we're a waitress, or a barista, or a lawyer, or a student. And we're not sure we like what it says!

Maybe you're thinking, "Sure, I'm a student, but I'm also a daughter, a singer, an artist, or a really good friend. *No seriously, you should see me.* I can adventure with the best of them, talk over coffee until the cows come home, soothe the brokenhearted like no one you've ever met. But none of that shows up in my job title." When someone asks us what we do, what exactly are they asking? What exactly should we tell them?

I'm learning the question has more leeway than I ever imagined. Just because I work at a coffee shop, or go to school part-time, or run the merchandise table on a fifty-state road trip doesn't mean I'm not *also* the things I've wanted to be all along. Sometimes who we are, just like the dreams we have, and the love we're building, needs to be called into existence before it can grow. Sometimes saying, "I'm a writer," is the first step.

The next morning I met with Eve from the nonprofit and gave her my resume, and she listened intently as I answered her questions. Then I drove the car back to the loft, and Sharaya and I sat on the couch, working together for the last time. Around noon, Sharaya ducked out to have lunch with a new friend. In the still of the apartment, I opened a blank document.

"It all started at a wedding," I wrote. "So many good stories do."

FAKE IT TILL YOU MAKE IT

Sharaya played her last show at Hotel Cafe, one of the hallmark venues for a new artist. We had invited everyone we knew who lived in the state of California, ignoring the fact that it was nearly nine hundred miles from top to bottom. As we prepared for the show, I noticed a difference in Sharaya. She was strangely calm. I didn't even have to encourage her this time. She just got up on stage, the red velvet curtain blazing behind her, and played the most beautiful show I had ever heard her play.

I wasn't the only one who noticed. As she stepped off stage several others complimented her on her composure and stage presence. One friend, who had moved from Portland to LA in the time we had been traveling, grabbed Sharaya by both arms and said, "You have grown so much since I saw you play six months ago."

Sharaya beamed. She was coming into herself as a woman and as an artist. It was fun to watch.

The next morning, we said goodbye to friends and to warm weather and climbed in our car to head north. We had exactly one week until Christmas.

"What do you think about faking it till you make it?" I asked Sharaya as we sped north on I-5 toward Medford.

"What do you mean?" she asked.

"At the party the other night, all I did was say I was a writer, and suddenly I had a job interview," I said. "What do you think about that? Do you think you can become something just by saying it out loud?"

"Ally, you're the only one who thinks you weren't a writer until you said it out loud. You're already a writer. Everyone knows it except for you."

Now that I look back, I see how right she was. Faking it till you make it doesn't really work. People who fake their way to the top have been faking it their whole lives. You can spot a faker from a mile away. Nobody likes fakers. They're arrogant, hard to get along with, and they're no fun. Their whole lives are ordered around protecting their fake identities. But there's a difference between faking it till you make it and being realistic about the person you already are.

The hard part is that it's not always easy to be honest about ourselves. First, there's our own insecurity to reckon with. We might think we're just being humble when we say, "I'm not really that good at anything," or "I don't have any expertise that's different from anyone else." We might think underplaying our skills and gifts is the right way to go. But I wonder if we're only stealing the joy others might have, and we might have, if we're just honest about who we are and what we have to offer. I wish I could pass off insecurity as a burden to bear and everyone would feel really sorry for me, but the more I think about it the more I see that my insecurity is really pride. My insecurity makes everything all about me.

Then there are the voices of others to contend with. We're called names in grade school, and we carry those things with us into adulthood. We believe all kinds of lies about ourselves, and those lies become part of our identities. Sometimes it's hard to silence the voices of our upbringing to tell the truth about ourselves. The ability to step outside of our own experience and to see the situation for what it really is, neither overplaying our strengths nor undershooting them, takes a lot of wisdom. In fact, I think that's what wisdom is—the ability to zoom out from where we're standing and see the larger picture.

How many people needed to call me a "writer" before I believed it? Did I need more confirmation? There comes a point where we don't need anyone to tell us who we are anymore, we just need to take the information we have and run with it.

LOOSE ENDS

In Medford, Oregon, we tied up loose ends. Sharaya's family lived there—her mom and dad, her two sisters and their husbands—and it was a natural rest stop on the way to Portland. We drove into town and straight to a Mexican restaurant for lunch, where everyone met me with hugs and more enthusiasm than you'd expect for a first time meeting. But the truth was they didn't feel as new to me as they were. They felt like tiny refractions of the girl I had come to know and love over the past six months.

"I don't know how you did it," her sister Nakesha laughed. "I love Sharaya, but I couldn't live in a car with her for six months."

We told stories and joked about both of our bad habits, and laughed in a way you do over memories, even bad ones. It felt natural that our journey would wind down here, with the people and in the place where Sharaya had grown up. After lunch we traveled back to Sharaya's sister's house where we divided the clothing and other possessions we'd accumulated along the way. Somehow, as we traveled, boundaries had merged. Everything we owned had come to feel like it was neither mine nor hers, but ours, shared together. I wondered if marriage was this way, and if this was like a divorce where you lay out all of your belongings on the floor in front of you and decide who gets to keep what, and who has to leave what behind.

We had burned about a hundred CDs together, and we separated those too.

"Remember this one?" I showed Sharaya the one she had burned back in Wisconsin, when she'd had a bad day. It was mostly Alanis Morisette. We laughed, and remembered, and bartered "this shirt" for "that one."

Then there was the car. Both of our names were on the title, and we had both invested equally in the payments. Should we sell it and take the money? Would we lose money if we sold it now? If we kept it, who would drive it?

Sharaya needed a car to get to Nashville, and I needed furniture. I had sold most of mine, and Sharaya's furniture was now filling my apartment back in Portland. We weren't sure if it was a fair trade financially—the furniture for the car—but it seemed like the most logical thing to do. So we agreed. She would take over payments on the car, but everything we had invested so far would be hers, and the furniture would be mine.

We talked about what would happen with Alaska and Hawaii. We'd always assumed this part of the trip would just magically happen, that some door would just open, and we'd walk through it all the way to Maui. But our magical door hadn't appeared, and now as we rounded the corner toward home, we wondered where we were going to get the money to fly to these two remaining destinations. Plus, it had always been our goal to be home by Christmas, which we were fast approaching. After some deliberation, we decided to let Alaska and Hawaii go for now, with the hope that those opportunities would come another day—a day when we could afford it. But for now, it was time to go home.

As we unpacked, each item reminded us of some moment from our trip.

We remembered the crazy guy in upstate New York who invited us to dinner and kept trying to get us to go back to his house with him. "I'm the most interesting person you'll ever meet!" he kept yelling to us over and over again as we raced to our car as fast as we could.

"Did he think we were actually going to go with him?" Sharaya asked, and I laughed so hard I almost fell off the couch where I was sitting.

We reminisced about Sharaya's friends Brooke and Joel in Montana—the perfect picture of a super model couple, the last people you'd expect to find living in a state like Montana. Brooke was gluten-free, and one night she cooked us dinner on the grill and almost burnt all of her blonde hair off.

"Remember Canada?" Sharaya asked.

I remembered. We had taken this last-minute detour from Detroit to Toronto, and back down into New York through Niagara Falls. When we tried to cross the border back into the United States we ran into some trouble because, despite our persistent paperwork, we still hadn't received the registration for our car. Imagine trying to explain to uptight border agents why you have two Oregon driver's licenses, a car you purchased in Wyoming, and a temporary registration from Nebraska. Needless to say, they asked us a thousand questions. But the falls had been so beautiful it made everything worth the trouble.

I thought about the picture we'd taken: the wind blowing our hair in our faces against the thick mist of the falls in the background.

"I'm so glad we did that. I've always wanted to see Niagara Falls."

"Me too," I said.

Memory after memory, we laid them out in front of us on the floor with all of our belongings—CDs, travel mugs, leftover postcards, and clothes. We sifted through them and came to silent agreements about them—which ones were worth keeping, how we would hold them, and where, and why. We tied up these loose ends together. For me, there were more loose ends than I was sharing, but they were unspoken. I wondered what would happen when I got home, if I would ever write the book I planned to write. I wondered if I would see Ben, if I would run into him in the grocery store somewhere with his new girlfriend, the one I had imagined so specifically that I could tell you the imaginary color of her imaginary hair.

But maybe he didn't have a girlfriend and I would run into him in a grocery store anyway. Maybe we would both be reaching for the same pasta sauce on the shelf. Maybe our meeting would be as serendipitous and beautiful as the first. And maybe, just maybe, his love for me wouldn't just be past tense. This is the problem with loose ends. Sometimes we don't want them to be tied up.

12

the mourning after

"When we get out of the glass bottle of our ego and when we escape like the squirrels in the cage of our personality and get into the forest again, we shall shiver with cold and fright. But things will happen to us so that we don't know ourselves. Cool, unlying life will rush in."

D. H. LAWRENCE

COMING HOME WAS LIKE stepping off a treadmill—you've been running for so long, you lose your balance when you finally stop. We drove on I-5 North, straight to I-405, and took the exit at Glisan Street. And it all came flooding back: the mess of brick buildings that is the Pearl District, the Rogue Brewery, the lighting store on the corner, and the The Lizard Lounge, an upscale clothing boutique, all went flashing by.

People marched along the sidewalks, in all their Portland strangeness, despite overcast skies and cold temperatures. One guy wore dress pants and a Marmott jacket with his hood up, no umbrella. We saw a young woman on her bike, in dress pants and running shoes. There were several women coming out of a nearby yoga studio, with their yoga mats in tow.

"Who's going to be there tonight?" Sharaya asked. We had planned a little last-minute reunion at one of our favorite restaurants in the Pearl District.

"Everyone," I said. We were both excited.

Our friends greeted us with hugs and smiles and a million questions about our trip. "Austin," we answered to "city that felt most like Portland." "New York," we said when they asked about the most exciting. "Laramie," we told them when they asked about the most terrifying experience of the trip.

"What was the most awful?"

"Losing my apartment," Sharaya said.

"Did you hear she got a booking at Hotel Cafe?" I asked, changing the subject so I wouldn't have to answer the same question.

It felt good to be home, but strange too. Erica's hair was longer, and Tyler was talking about the new house where he was living. Rebecca looked beautiful in her new leather jacket. A new couple had formed in our friend group. And we had missed all of it.

The hardest part of it all was that Ben wasn't there. I had imagined this moment for so long, pictured what it would look like to touch him and hug him again, to see this one person I had missed the most. In every scenario I had rehearsed of my homecoming, he had been there. But he wasn't.

And I know I shouldn't have done this, but I did. I should have just left the whole thing alone. But I got out my phone and sent him a text message: "Can we meet up to trade stuff?"

The conversation unfolded around me and I sank into it, like a warm comforter at the end of the day. I let it wrap its arms around me and draw me in. I was different now. Different than I was before I left. I had experienced things they hadn't, things I may never fully be able to explain, and the same had happened for them. When I drove home with Rebecca that night I felt it—the thing I had worried about so much before I left. Life had gone on without us while we were away.

LOST ITEMS

Ben met me at a coffee shop near my neighborhood to do our final exchange of stuff—you know, that unpleasant business you usually do a week or so after a breakup. I couldn't tell if he was humoring me, or if he really wanted to do this. As for me, I was ambivalent. One moment, I couldn't wait to see him. In the next moment, I hated him, seethed at him for changing his mind and breaking my heart.

From the minute I saw him, I knew everything was different. Here we were, only blocks from where we had sat months ago, dreaming of our life together when I returned, and now we couldn't be further apart. I had spent months dreaming about the moment I would see him again, and now this was it. This was the end.

"I brought your stuff," I told him, and handed him the bag. He handed over his own collection of my things. And then we sat there for a few minutes, silent, awkward.

"How was your trip?" he asked.

"It was fine," I said.

"I read the blog," he told me.

"I sat up every night thinking about you," I wanted to say, "wondering why you told me I was the one you wanted, and then changed your mind. I wondered if there was something wrong with me. I told myself that I was beautiful, and that I didn't do anything wrong, and that, someday, someone will love me too. But I'm having a hard time hanging on to that conclusion."

But I didn't say any of that. I don't remember what we said—probably because I was too busy thinking about what we weren't saying. After a few minutes of meaningless dialogue, I left—without even ordering a coffee.

I drove home crying, not just because of Ben, but because home didn't feel like home anymore and I wasn't sure what to do to get back to the life I had before. Maybe there was no way to do that. Maybe that's what happens when you move forward: you sacrifice the possibility that life will ever be the way it was before. Maybe this is what happens when you go on a road trip, or start a new relationship, or follow a passion, or walk the road to maturity. Maybe there is no going back.

WAS IT WORTH IT?

While Rebecca was at work, I went through our apartment and made piles of stuff I thought we should get rid of. It was a little unfair, since it was more her apartment than it was mine, and most of the stuff I was piling belonged to her. But I had been running so fast for so long, I couldn't seem to bring myself to slow down. With no more shows to book, no more press releases to write, no more worrying about where we were going to be staying the next night, or how many people were going to turn up at a show, I just started finding tasks to keep myself busy.

If I slowed down physically, my mind would start to spin with things I had learned while we were gone. And how was I going to implement those lessons in my everyday life now? I couldn't just go back to the way it was before, could I? Then everything would really be lost. I wasn't sure what packing light lessons really looked like in my everyday life, but I knew I had to try.

Even when every cabinet and drawer had been sorted and there were piles all over the house of hair products and cleaning products and old clothes, something still didn't feel right. The restlessness I felt before I left was still there. And I was starting to panic because this was supposed to be the trip to cure that restlessness. If the restlessness was still with me, it had to be more about me than about my circumstances. I wasn't sure what to do about that.

I would lie awake at night, just like I had on the trip, wondering what it all meant and who was going to help me figure it out. Sharaya was leaving for Nashville, where she was going to be doing what she's always wanted to do. She was living out the very thing she'd quit her job, sold her car, and got rid of all her stuff for. This road trip was my idea, and yet I didn't have any idea on the other side of it how I was going to write a book or write anything, for that matter. I had given up everything, and what did I get in return?

Should I get a job? Should I keep writing? Should I go back to teaching? Should I move? What was the culmination of all of this? How could I make it worth it? I didn't have answers to any of these questions, and they kept me up at night.

If I couldn't figure it out, I could at least update our blog and pretend I had it all together. I prepared a "We're home!" post, typed in the password, and got an error message. So I tried again—another error message. Then again—a third error message.

"This password has been changed by the user," it said.

I called Sharaya.

"Did you change the password to the Packing Light blog?" I asked.

"Yeah, why?" she asked.

"I was trying to upload a post today and couldn't log in." There was a pause on the other end of the line.

"When are you going to start your own blog, Ally?"

"Excuse me?"

"We've been using my blog, which was great for the purpose of the trip, but I'm just wondering when you're going to start your own blog."

Silently, I dropped the phone to my side and hit the "end" button.

I shouldn't have done it. I knew I shouldn't have. It wasn't Sharaya's fault I was feeling the way I was feeling, but it was so much easier to feel mad at her than it was to feel mad at myself for thinking that I could take the easy way out, riding on the coattails of her success, her progress, her adulthood. It all came flooding back— the months I had spent as an outlier, as a cheerleader to someone else. In some ways I wondered if I was still doing that. Why *hadn't* I started my own blog? It wasn't because I was such a nice person, or because I was really selfless. It was because I was scared.

I had gone on a stupid road trip but nothing had changed. Here I was, six months later, having "risked everything" to go, but having risked nothing at the very same time. I couldn't go back, but I also didn't feel like I could go forward. I was stuck.

I called Sharaya back and told her my feelings were really hurt. I cried and told her that I knew it was selfish, but that I wanted her to be for me what I was for her—the cheerleader standing on the sidelines, telling me that I was amazing, and that everything was going to be okay.

"I feel really under-supported," I told her.

"What have you done that I haven't supported?" she asked.

I wanted to punch her for saying it, the way we always want to punch people when they say something we know is right. I knew what she was saying. She was saying what I already knew was true: I hadn't done anything yet. I hadn't written a book. I hadn't even started my own blog. In some ways, everything had changed, and in some ways, nothing had. I was stalling.

It took me a long time to see that Sharaya was supporting me in her own way—in a way I had never supported her. She was pushing me out. No, she didn't sit next to me while I wrote blog posts to remind me how amazing everyone thought I was. And no, it didn't feel very good at the time. But in some ways, she was more supportive to me than anyone else ever was. She told me the truth about myself, as she saw it. And it meant I had to change the way I was living.

As long as you're a spectator in your life, you're not a worshiper of God. You can be an obedient spectator, but not a worshiping spectator. So many of us are living our lives like this. I certainly was— I was a spectator to what was happening around me. It's safer that way. It's easier that way. But you can't worship when you're sitting on your hands. You're not worshiping unless you're *doing* something.

It's like Sharaya asking me to dance at the wedding. I had to put down my glass of wine, get over my pride, and get into the mess of the party. That was the only way to make friends, the only way to learn, the only way to be a part of the story.

If you want to be a worshiper of God, you've got to do something with what you've been given. What you decide to do, that's up to you. It might be a colossal mistake, or it might be a huge success. Or it might be somewhere in the middle. But no matter what it is, it's better than doing nothing at all.

Think about the parable of the talents. A man goes on a journey and entrusts his wealth to three of his servants. To one servant, he gives three talents. To another, he gives five. And to another servant he gives one talent. The man with five talents invests his, and doubles his investment. The man with three does the same, and sees the same results. The man with only one talent buries his in the sand to protect it, and presents the man the same talent he was given before the journey. The owner of the talents only gets mad at one guy—and it's the guy who buried his talent in the sand.

Worshiping always involves doing. It means getting your hands dirty. It means being vulnerable and open and sometimes hurt by people who break your heart or call you names. It means dancing when you don't know how. It means telling jokes that fall flat, writing things you'll later find embarrassing. It means making lots of mistakes. It means living the kind of life where every little thing doesn't tie up perfectly at the end.

This is the kind of life that makes us a worshiper. It's the kind of life where we can't help but end each day with our hands lifted high, thanking God for the ways He graciously accepts even our worst mistakes, the way He uses every experience to teach us, the way He wiggles His way into the story we're writing.

NEW BEGINNINGS

I convinced Rebecca we should move. I know it sounds crazy since we were happy where we were, but I just felt like it was time for a new beginning. It was time to get out of the suburbs and into the city. It was time to get into the mess of things.

We found an apartment downtown that would be perfect for us. She forgave me for trying to make her get rid of a bunch of stuff that was perfectly useful, and we packed our boxes. On New Year's Eve, in the midst of a very rare snow flurry in the city of Portland, we moved to an adorable little duplex by the University of Portland. It had wood floors and crown molding and you had to climb a huge flight of stairs to get to the front door.

It was the perfect place to become a writer, I decided.

In January, we waved goodbye to Sharaya as she pulled out of our driveway and started her trip to Nashville. She had come over to exchange the last of her stuff, and to drop off some things that wouldn't fit in her car. I told her I was proud of her.

I worked part-time for the school district, substitute teaching when it was needed and taking writing jobs as they came up. I found a document about how to write a book proposal, and put one together titled *Packing Light: A Guide to Living Life with Less Baggage*. I did the best I could. I practiced telling people "I'm a writer," and each time it got a little bit easier.

Each morning I wasn't teaching I would get up and walk to the closest coffee shop. I would order a black coffee and sit for a few hours with my computer until I started to feel hungry for lunch. I started a blog, my own blog, and began writing whatever was on my mind.

Some mornings I would sit and write blog posts and then delete them completely before they were ever published. Maybe it's a good thing I never shared those thoughts with the world. Maybe it was my better sense kicking in, telling me that there were some things I should process before publishing, and some things that were better off just kept to myself. But I can't help but wonder if it was healthy how worked up I got about a blog post. It reminded me of Sharaya getting on stage to play her songs.

"You're fine," I would tell her. "People love you."

But no matter how many times I said it, I couldn't get her to take it to heart.

We were both desperate for someone to tell us that we were okay, that we were going to make it, that we were loved no matter what. I wished I had had someone to sit next to me while I wrote blog posts and contacted publishers, the way Sharaya had every night before she went up on stage. But then again, even if

I had that, it probably wouldn't have helped. Even if they said it, I wouldn't have believed them. I had to come to that conclusion myself.

I wonder if it's this way for many of us—if we're waiting for someone to tell us how valuable we really are, to convince us to unbury our talent, to come out and share our great wealth with the world. And I wonder if this is what taking a trip is all about. Even the kind of trip where we never leave home. I wonder if the ups and the downs of traveling, the highs and the lows, are all just part of the process. I wonder if they're just mile-markers on the journey to discovering how much we matter, how valuable we really are, and how much we have to give.

13

three feet from gold

"Only time will tell what we'll find when we lose ourselves;
what may come, we can't know for sure,
but we'll keep digging deep."
SHARAYA MIKAEL

KNOWING HOW VALUABLE YOU are, and acknowledging your tiny role in a larger story is a difficult balance to strike. It's easy to see one or the other, but it's difficult to hang on to both at the same time. It stretches us, like a kid reaching for the next rung of a monkey bar, until eventually we find our arms spread out wide.

Each day we go through a routine. Whether we're on a fifty-state road trip, or at home with our kids, or going to school to get a degree, we have one. We have places we go and things we do and people who, even if we've never met, we brush shoulders with on a regular basis—the checker at the grocery store, the woman talking loud on her cell phone at the bank. Our lives are made up of rhythms and cycles, seasons and systems spinning, and we are just one piece in the puzzle. It's easy to get lost in all of it, fading into the background, or to find a way to feel like our piece is more important than everyone else's. We don't mean any harm. We just get tunnel vision.

After Sharaya left, it was easy to get lost in my own piece of the puzzle and fall out of touch with her, even though our story wasn't finished. It was the path of least resistance. I was doing my thing, she was doing hers. We were busy. Our lives were full. There wasn't much time to talk, or to think about how we still had two more states to visit.

"Are you guys still friends?" people would always ask, with this sympathetic look on their face like they were sure I was going to say no.

But we were still friends. We were friends the way you have to be friends with people who live thousands of miles away: tied together with memories of the past and hope for the future.

There was a kind of relief we felt, I think, in not having someone every day put our patience and insecurities to the test. It was the way you feel after a hard workout, a deep breath like: "Phew, that was good, but I'm glad it's over." But Sharaya had changed me. I was different forever.

I was a little more open, more adventurous, more certain good things were going to happen. It was me doing the convincing these days, the way Sharaya had convinced me to dance at the wedding. I convinced Rebecca to leave the house at night, to stay out a little later than usual, to take a few more chances, to wander down to Powell's during the filming of the *Blue Like Jazz* movie to see if we could be extras on set. I was a different woman. The journey had changed me. Sharaya had changed me. That's what friends do, I think.

Of course, there were times I wondered how you were supposed to be whimsical and adventurous given your current circumstance. I would be sitting in a classroom full of high school students, trying to convince them to stay in their seats and keep their eyes off their neighbor's paper, when it would occur to me how strange it was that this is what I was doing after a fifty-state road trip. Is this why I had given up everything? To come home and be a part-time version of what I was before?

I wondered if this is what the "rich young ruler" was worried about when Jesus asked him to sell everything he owned. I wonder if this is what most of us are worried about when it comes to packing light. We're worried we'll get to the end of the journey and we'll be worse off than we were at the beginning.

I started reading blogs, especially blogs about being a writer, and tried the things they suggested. I worked on my book proposal, slowly but surely. On days I didn't teach I would sit by myself at our apartment, trying to pin words down to paper.

I would try things the experts suggested: writing every day, writing about different subjects, tracking my traffic. I experimented with lists, and stories, and subject matters I had never written about before. Some of it was strategic, some of it was spontaneous, and most of it was just trial and error. I watched traffic climb, slowly but surely. I watched readers from the Packing Light blog show up at my new blog. I watched the readership grow outside of my family and friends.

One Saturday, on a whim, I wrote a post about how much it bothered me that dating was so confusing. I would watch couples at my church and marvel at the way they would talk *around* the subject of dating for so long before they ever spoke to it. The post was straight from my gut, unfiltered and unedited, and maybe even a little unadvised. Regardless, I hit the "publish" button and watched the comments rush in. Turns out I wasn't the only one who felt this way.

It was fun—writing something that got everybody thinking and talking. It was about me, but it wasn't at the same time. It was just being honest. There was no hype, no fifty-state road trip, no trying to make everything sound safe but exciting. It was just the regular, everyday stuff I was thinking and feeling.

Then one night, in spite of pressing insecurity, I gathered the courage and wrote a post called "The 10 Biggest Mistakes I've Made in Dating." And although I hovered over the "publish" button for several minutes before pulling the trigger, I finally did it. It was like jumping off the waterfall in Costa Rica—terrifying at first and then exhilarating.

If I had stopped to think if the post made me sound like a "Christian" writer I might not have done it. Instead, I just told the truth. I stopped worrying about what everyone was going to say, or how it made me sound, and simply was myself. I stopped performing and wrote from my brokenness. I wrote what was on my heart.

I still remember the first email I received, thanking me for my story. I had shared about a time in college when I had stayed in a bad relationship too long, and she could identify with that. Reading my story, she said, helped her release the tight grip regret and shame had held in her life.

"I thought those things had a hold on me," she told me. "What I didn't realize is that I had a hold on them. I always had the ability to set them down."

"Packing light," I whispered into the glowing computer screen.

That's when I began to see it—the thing I pointed out to Sharaya, back in Ann Arbor—the place where my passion intersected with the response of others.

CLARIFYING THE VISION

From the outside, my life didn't look bigger or more powerful than it had before. I took writing jobs that paid next to nothing.

I didn't have a car, so I had to take public transportation to any teaching jobs, which added sometimes two hours onto each work day. Between teaching and writing, I was making barely enough to pay my rent, so I applied for food stamps and was accepted. I wished for things like a prettier winter coat or a new pair of boots, and beautiful curtains to hang over the windows where I sat in the mornings, staring out over the city. I still hadn't heard from a single publisher. I wondered if I ever would.

On the outside, I wondered if I should just walk away and go get another full-time teaching job. But on the inside, everything was different. Everything had changed. Something was stirring up, and I could feel it.

"Maybe I should just get a nine-to-five again," I told Rebecca one night as we were hanging our photos and mirrors (most of which were hers) in our new place. She listened, and nodded, and tried not to give me her opinion, I'm sure.

"I think you should do what you think is right," she said. I wished I knew what was right. I wished she would tell me. I set the small nails and brackets I was holding down on a small end table and sat down on what used to be Sharaya's couch. I buried my face in my hands. Then I suddenly looked up.

"Do you think it was worth it?" I asked.

"Do I think what was worth it?"

"The road trip," I said.

She dropped the hammer she was holding to her side, and sat down next to me. "Why do you ask?" she said.

I looked around our apartment, and motioned to myself, the tattered sweats I was wearing, and the knot of hair tied up high on top of my head.

"I have nothing," I told her.

"You have more than you think you do."

"Like what?"

"Like your blog, like an experience that most other people will never have. And besides, you're different than before you left."

"You think so?" I asked.

"I know so," she said.

She stood up and reached out her hand, silently asking for another nail and bracket so she could finish hanging a photo of her grandparents.

"What are you writing about on the blog tomorrow?" she asked.

"It's called 'The Best Piece of Dating Advice I've Ever Received.'"

I laced the nail through the bracket and handed it to her. She positioned it carefully and gave it a firm whack with the hammer.

The advice came from Melissa, a mutual friend of ours, and it went something like this: dating is clarifying the vision. Each time you go on a date, you get a clearer picture of what you want in a wife or husband. Maybe the date is a total bore, or maybe he's a jerk. Maybe you decide never to go out with him again. But no matter what you decide about the guy, or how long you date him, the time isn't lost. He helps you clarify your vision. No matter how disastrous the date or the relationship, you always know that there was purpose in it. It teaches you something.

Rebecca gave a few more small taps with her hammer and then reached out for another nail and bracket.

"Do you notice how excited you get when you talk about writing?" she asked. "Your whole posture changes, your whole demeanor."

Her words sank deep into me, satisfying a need I didn't even know I had. They helped me silence the shame, the feelings of failure, the wandering thoughts that maybe I had heard God wrong when He told me He would be with me, or that everything was going to be okay.

Rebecca's words were so simple, but what I heard was, "You thought the point was to write a book, but even if you never hear from a single publisher, give yourself some credit. You did it. You took the leap. And you're a different person than you were before."

Rebecca gave two last taps of the hammer and balanced the photo carefully before stepping back to admire her handiwork.

"Clarifying the vision," she repeated. "Sounds like advice for more than just dating."

Sometimes I think we get hung up on objectives, and it makes us too hard on ourselves. If we think the objective is to get a certain job, or a certain car, or a certain spouse, then of course we'll feel like a failure when that doesn't happen. Of course we'll wonder if we heard God wrong, or if we made a wrong turn somewhere. But what if the point isn't the end product? Or what if the end product isn't what we thought it was? What if the point is the trip, and the end product is us?

THE THINGS YOU LEARN

Since I was always blogging about dating, my church asked me to live-blog for an event called Loveology: The Theology of Love and Sex for Young Adults. I didn't know what live-blogging was, but it sounded fun, so I agreed. Basically, they told me, I was just supposed to sit at the event quoting updates, thoughts, and maybe some questions for people to answer. The goal was to engage as many people as possible.

While I sat to the side of the stage, I thought about Sharaya and how often I sat at her concerts doing this exact same thing. It's amazing the things you learn without even realizing it.

After the second night ended, I drove home in a car I had borrowed while my friend was out of town for the weekend. It was nearly eleven when my phone rang and I picked it up.

"Hello?"

"Is this Ally?" the caller asked.

"Yes," I said.

"I hope I didn't catch you too late. This is time-sensitive. I'm wondering if you would like to go to Hawaii."

I caught my breath.

He explained that he was the president of a company called Everlasting Tours, and they were hosting a marriage conference in Maui that summer. He said he'd gotten my name from Sharaya, who he'd hired to lead worship on the trip. He had read my blog, he said, and seen some of the things I had written and was really impressed. "So anyway," he concluded. "Do you have any experience live-blogging?"

"Actually, yes!" I said.

"Okay, then we need to book your ticket tonight."

This is the part of clarifying the vision that amazes me the most, I think. It's also the reason outcomes get us off track. We get so focused on what we think is going to happen, so worried about it, we don't even consider something better might be coming, something we couldn't have possibly dreamed up ourselves. It's like Deadwood reaching out its hand to us in the middle of South Dakota, or the free yoga classes at the Arizona resort. It pops up out of nowhere. It disrupts our simple, regular life. And whether it's an invitation to Hawaii, a bustling town filled with bikers from Australia, a job offer we never expected, or a friend showing up on our doorstep at just the right moment, it never fails to teach us that we shouldn't assume we know what's coming.

THE GRAND WAILEA

As Sharaya and I prepared for our trip to Hawaii, we thought about how we could make Alaska happen at the same time. It only made sense. Sharaya would already be on this side of the country. She wouldn't have to buy another ticket from Nashville at another time.

"I don't have any money," I told her over the phone. "None."

"Things are really tight for me too."

So we tried to get creative. We sold some things on Craigslist. We asked our parents if they would chip in. We put the word out on Facebook that we were trying to book flights, and a few friends offered to gift us airline miles. A friend of mine from college said she and her husband lived in Anchorage now. We could stay with them, and they would feed us, find us a place to play shows, and drive us around.

"It takes a village!" I joked with Sharaya as the whole thing unfolded. It was only appropriate we should finish this trip the same way we started—with a community of people helping us see it through to the end.

With all the travel booked, I packed my bags for two weeks in Hawaii, the warmest climate in the United States, and Alaska, the coldest climate. I packed sundresses and a leather jacket, my bathing suit, and a few colorful scarves.

"It's all about layers," Sharaya told me, the phone pressed to my ear as I folded items and placed them in my suitcase. "Layers and similar tones."

The next morning I climbed on a plane from Portland to Maui to finish the journey Sharaya and I had started almost a year ago, together.

We met in the front lobby of Grand Wailea, one of the most luxurious resorts in Hawaii. We laughed and hugged and gushed about how amazing this whole place was—so big it took us at least twenty minutes to walk from the entrance to our room in another wing. There was white marble and high arches and fountains, and of course a beautiful ocean view. I asked her about Nashville. She told me that it was scary and amazing, that she was making new friends and writing music and waiting tables to help make ends meet.

"It isn't glamorous," she said.

"But this is!" I replied, looking around the hallway.

While we stood outside of our hotel room, fumbling with our room key, I noticed there was a doorbell on the outside left wall. But before I could go through the whole process in my mind about why on earth you would need a doorbell on a hotel room, and how I had never even lived in an apartment big enough to need a doorbell, the double doors swung open and we stepped into the Presidential Suite. *This isn't a hotel room,* I thought to myself. *This is a hotel house.* I had never seen anything like it.

"Troy told me we're sharing with a few other staff members," Sharaya told me. "I guess we just pick whichever bedroom we want?"

"There are multiple bedrooms?" I squealed.

"Multiple bedrooms, bathrooms, and balconies," she said.

I walked around the room, gawking, sort of stumbling, wondering how on earth my substitute-teaching, food-stamp life had turned into this. *How was I here? How did I get to experience this? What had I done to deserve this?* I wondered.

Before I could finish exploring, Sharaya told me to grab my purse and follow her upstairs. We met Troy and he gave us the rundown for what he wanted us to do that week. I sat across from him at a table and took notes while he explained.

My main job would be to live-blog the event, which I had done exactly one other time, if you didn't count the fifty times I had done it for Sharaya. So I was practically an expert. He would also like me to interview artists and speakers, he said, and gave me a list of people to interview and questions I should ask.

"Set up a time with each of them separately," he said. "Any time all week, whatever works for them."

So for the next seven days I worked, but I also did yoga on the beach, went to a luau, laid out by the pool, played beach volleyball, listened to Sharaya play music, ate incredible breakfasts at the Napua Tower—which I found out later was supposed to be reserved for guests who spent more than $100,000 in their visit—and woke up to watch the sunrise as I wrote on the back balcony. In fact, as I sat writing one of two final blog posts for Packing Light, it all started to come together—this thing I couldn't have planned for myself.

This couldn't be happening, could it?

I'm learning that life is like this, most of the time. We struggle, we put our noses to the grindstone, we stay up late and get up early, and work as hard as we can. We worry that all our work is in vain. And then, one day, we show up, and things just start to happen. They aren't always good things all the time, but if we opt out because we're afraid of the bad stuff, or the neutral stuff, or the boring stuff, we'll never get to the good stuff. It's all part of the package. Who knew that food stamps and my stay at the Grand Wailea would happen in the same chapter?

It's easy to think, when you read the story of the "rich young ruler," that the answer is to get rid of all your stuff. But I think that's missing the point. I don't think God hates our stuff, even our nice stuff. I don't think He's mad at me for enjoying my stay at the Grand Wailea. Sometimes the luxuries we experience are as important to our journey as our discomfort. To say that the answer to living life to the fullest is just giving up all our stuff is giving our "stuff" way too much credit.

There is another story in the Gospels, immediately after the one about the "rich young ruler," about a man named Zacchaeus. Zacchaeus is a tax collector, and also very wealthy, just like the "rich young ruler." He is also curious about Jesus, so curious, that he climbs up in a tree just to see Him. I wonder if he wanted to ask Jesus a question like the "rich young ruler" did, or if he just wanted to be with Him. Either way, Jesus calls Zacchaeus down from the tree, and asks if He can come to his house and have dinner with him.

People thought Jesus was crazy for going to Zacchaeus's house for dinner. He was a rich man, and he'd gotten that way by cheating other people out of their money. It's really easy to hate people like that, and to assume that there is no way they'll ever experience a single taste of heaven.

But Zacchaeus, out of nowhere, tells Jesus that he's going to give up half of what he owns and give it to the poor. Not all of it—half of it. And Jesus tells him that he has found salvation. Why did Jesus tell the "rich young ruler" to sell everything, and yet Zacchaeus only had to sell half? Depending on how rich Zacchaeus was, half of "really rich" is probably still pretty wealthy.

Because Jesus doesn't care about our stuff nearly as much as we do. He doesn't hate our stuff. In fact, often He likes to bless us with it—just like He did with Sharaya and me at the Grand Wailea, just like I'm sure He's done with you. He wants you to enjoy your nice house, or your heated seats, or your loving parents if you have them. He just doesn't want the stuff to become the point. Because when stuff becomes the point of our life, we miss out on the greatest blessing of all: the freedom we feel when we're fully engaged in the push-pull of life, the letting go, and the holding on.

I COULDN'T HAVE KNOWN

We couldn't have known Hawaii was going to be as good as it was, and the best part about embracing the unknown is that it teaches you. It clarifies your vision. It's your Deadwood—giving you hope that something good is coming.

"I want to fly a plane when we're in Alaska," I told Sharaya as we flew toward Anchorage. We were strapped into our seats and the flight attendant had just handed Sharaya a half-sized Diet Coke.

"One of those little prop planes?" Sharaya asked.

"Yeah!" I got excited as I talked about it and sat straight up in my seat. I reached over her to grab my own Diet Coke and the tiny bag of trail mix.

We talked about life after the road trip. It was good, we agreed, but nothing like we expected. Most people would say things like "It must be hard to come back from something as dramatic as a fifty-state road trip and settle back into boring, everyday life."

No, I would think to myself. *That's not it.* It's more like it's hard to come back from something as challenging as a fifty-state road trip and learn that *all* of life is that challenging, when we choose to engage it. If we want to be truly alive, truly awake to the reality of the world around us, packing light will be a continued, daily struggle. That was the hard part, if you asked me: waking up to the reality that most of life isn't glamorous. But when we're willing to wade through the grit of it, rather than standing on the sidelines hoping not to get hurt, you get to experience Deadwoods, kind words, free sandwiches from those who are moved by what you're doing, and even luxuries like the Grand Waileas.

Life, if we're being honest with ourselves, will be a little bit like brushing your teeth from a water bottle and eating breakfast from a plastic yogurt container out of a cooler in your backseat. There will be dirty laundry, and it will be virtually impossible to keep up with all of your email, and it will be really easy to fall into a routine. But then, out of nowhere, there will be Deadwood, South Dakota, and Friendship, Maine, and the thrill of New York City—that is, if we haven't checked out already.

Sharaya and I sat still for a moment, just enjoying our Diet Cokes and the roar of the jet engine.

"I think sometimes when things get hard, too many of us assume we're moving the wrong direction," she told me. "Like if we're doing life right, it's supposed to be easy."

I nodded.

I couldn't help but think about how I was as guilty of this as anyone. I wouldn't have said it out loud, but this was the way I was living my life, before the road trip at least, if not after. I was living like it was going to get easy one of these days if I just kept following all the directions. I had bartered with God: promised that if He did something for me, I would do something for Him, and the same was true the other way around. If I did something for Him, He had better do something for me back. It wasn't two people giving freely and openly. It wasn't a relationship; it was a business partnership. It was cold and stilted, when I allowed it to be.

I think we all go through seasons like this with God. It's a relationship, after all, and relationships go through rich and dry spells. It takes some time to figure out how to abandon yourself to someone, or to something, to trust in it completely—even if it is completely trustworthy. I wonder how many of us aren't *leaning* yet, not totally anyway, into what we know to be true about Him. He's shown up when no one else did, carried us through an experience that threatened to steal us from the inside out, healed us, and put us back together when we didn't even know we were broken. I wonder what it will take for us to finally decide it's worth it.

The plane started to descend, and the mountains below us got bigger and bigger. The mountains weren't covered in snow, but they were capped in it, and everything was this electric shade of unearthly blue, green, and white.

We deplaned in Anchorage and made our way to baggage claim. My friend Amanda picked us up at the airport and drove us to her favorite place for lunch, and then to meet her husband. They graciously drove us around to show us the scenery—from open fields with prop planes to lakes that seemed to disappear into glaciers, to glaciers that opened wide to meet the sky. It was as if there was no end to Alaska or its natural beauty.

"I want to fly a prop plane," I told Amanda and Ryan in the car.

"We could probably make that happen," Ryan said. "There are companies around here that take tourists up all the time. If that doesn't work, I can call a few friends who are pilots."

Sharaya started researching prices from her phone, and Ryan called his friends. In between phone calls and websites we would get out to look at a lake that stretched itself out across the countryside, bright with the light of day even though it was six at night. As we drove over remote dirt roads winding through the Alaskan landscape, we saw several people tending to their personal airplanes.

"Lovely day for a flight lesson!" I joked from the backseat.

"I dare you to ask one of them," Sharaya said.

"Do it!" Ryan said.

It seemed like something Sharaya would have done on our road trip—getting out of the car to ask a perfect stranger if he would teach us how to fly his plane sometime. But before I knew it, it was me who was speaking up, not Sharaya, pulling the sweetest, nicest voice I could muster and saying things like, "It's our first time in Alaska. Who knows if we'll ever be able to come back?"

I couldn't have known he would say yes before I asked him, especially since he seemed a little hesitant at first, even frustrated that I had trespassed on his property. But slowly the conversation went from, "I wasn't planning to go up today" to "I actually am a flight instructor" to "Maybe just for an hour." Before we knew it, we were taking off in the tiny plane, flying over glaciers and forests.

You never know what will happen when you get out of the car, or out of your seat, and ask a question.

It's like the email I sent while I was sitting in Amanda and Ryan's living room later that evening. I had been meaning to do it for quite some time but had been putting it off because I was scared of rejection. I was scared for someone to tell me I wasn't good enough, or didn't have what it takes.

It was a simple request: Can I guest post on your blog? Every blogging expert I had ever read recommended this very simple practice: guest post for other blogs. So I uploaded my sample post, hit the "send" button, and crossed my fingers that Jeff Goins would like it. I couldn't have known before I asked that he would use it, and that someone very important would read it. Not a publisher, like I was hoping, but someone even better—my future husband.

I couldn't have imagined that Darrell Vesterfelt, a man who I would later come to love and trust, would read my article on Jeff Goins's blog and say to himself: "I have to meet this girl." I couldn't have known. My imagination isn't that good.

It would be so much easier if we knew these things before we took the leap, wouldn't it? It would make it so much easier to jump if we knew everything was going to turn out okay. It would be so much easier if we knew exactly how the journey was going to turn out before we started. It would be nicer if we had a budget and a plan, if we knew steps eight, nine, and ten before we started step one. But sometimes I think we have to take the first few steps before the next ones are uncovered. It's not like God is playing chicken with us; it's just that He wants us to lean into Him, to trust ourselves a little more and to trust Him.

14

write your own book

"A book, too, can be a star, a living fire to lighten the darkness, leading out into the expanding universe."

MADELINE L'ENGLE

I CAME HOME FROM Hawaii and Alaska with a renewed sense of confidence, a reminder of what it felt like to lean into life, to hold nothing back. Summer was coming in Portland and the sun was finally coming out and people were coming out of their Marmott cocoons to enjoy long evenings with no rain. There was a sort of energy buzzing around my writing, a building momentum. I had taken a couple of risks, and I hadn't been rejected. It gave me just enough confidence to ask one more question.

One of the speakers I interviewed in Hawaii was Gary Thomas, the author of *Sacred Marriage* and about a dozen other books. During the interview I asked Gary and his wife, Lisa, the questions Troy had given me, but as we talked it felt less like an interview and more like a conversation. They reminded me of my own parents, and I felt relaxed and safe talking with them. I mentioned how I did some writing too, and that I had a blog, and before I knew it we were exchanging information.

"Stay in touch," Gary told me.

So when the idea came to me one day, the way ideas tended to do, Gary was the first person I thought of. *I should write a dating book,* I thought. After all, my blog had basically turned into a dating blog, and I knew there was a lot of interest around it. My website was free research for what young people wanted to talk about when it came to dating. The numbers would soar above normal when I wrote a post that really struck a chord with my generation. Perhaps because I was writing it, and living it. I was right in the mix of things.

So I composed the email with great care, thinking through all possible reservations Gary might have about letting someone else write a book for him. I made sure to cover all my bases, without being too wordy (writers are busy, and they hate getting wordy emails from pandering fans, I told myself.) But I told him I wanted to write his next book for him. It could be called *Sacred Dating,* which would fit right in with *Sacred Marriage* and *Sacred Parenting.* I would write the book for just a small percentage, and I didn't even need to have my name on it. I offered to write the proposal for free, and even the manuscript. I laid out all my chapter ideas and the title, which I thought was particularly brilliant, and I figured there was no way Gary could possibly turn it down. He didn't have to do any work. I would do everything. Then I took a deep breath and hit "send."

A week later, his response showed up in my inbox. It was a rather long email, but I read quickly because I was so anxious to get to the important part. I scanned through the paragraphs and then arrived at his answer: "Too many young authors waste their energy on books for someone else. I think your idea is a good one, but you need to write your own book."

It was the best rejection I had ever received in my entire life, and one I'll pass on to as many people as I can in my lifetime. I'll do my best to make sure I'm the kind of person who doesn't try to steal energy from other people to promote my cause or my message. Because my message is important, but it's important mostly because it's mine. You have a message too, and it's important because it's yours.

It's not bad to partner with someone else to promote their vision. It's part of living life in community, learning from one another, and celebrating our values. It's a gift we can give each other, to learn from one another as we do life together, to share our energy so that each of our ideas can become a reality. But there's a difference between giving someone your time and giving up.

It's too easy to give up on our own ideas because we're afraid they'll never happen. We don't have enough followers on Twitter. No publisher would ever notice us, so we might as well ride the coattails of someone else. It's too easy to think that someone with more friends, more influence, a bigger platform, a bigger church, is doing something better than you and you should just jump on their bandwagon. But if we spend our whole lives jumping on other people's bandwagons, the world misses out on what we have to offer. We miss out too.

My friend Matt says that your whole life is a work of art, and that you get to choose what it looks like. You can choose to make it beautiful or mediocre. You can make it look like everyone else's, or you can say, "Forget it, I give up," before you're actually finished. If your life is a piece of art—what would it look like?

If you feel like you have nothing to say, or like you do but that it couldn't possibly matter to anyone, don't give up. It's too easy to just serve someone else's vision. I did this with Sharaya, and I did it with Gary Thomas, and I'm so glad they were both wise enough to push me out, to challenge me to pursue my own calling, to make my own piece of art. I hope I'm rejected a thousand times over if this is what rejection does. I hope you're rejected a thousand times over it if it means your ideas won't get lost in the mix of life, if it means that they won't die with you. After all, you're the only one who has your ideas, your legacy. If you don't do something about them, no one will.

CAN I WRITE ABOUT THIS?

I wondered what people would think if I wrote about all of this. I wondered how I could write about losing Ben without losing it myself. I wondered how I could write about my anger at God and still be a Christian author, how I could write about a conflict with Sharaya and still be a faithful friend. I wondered if Sharaya would let me write about Sam, and if I should tell the story about Will, or about staying with Gus in New York. If I wrote about it would people think we were being reckless? Would they be able to understand?

When it came to writing blog posts about our trip, I worded them carefully. I made sure to tell the best parts of stories, to always make them seem safer than they were. There was no use in making people worry unnecessarily. We were fine. But if I was going to write a book, I wanted to tell the real stories. If I wrote about it in a book, it would be etched on paper forever.

This was the hardest part of writing: if we write it as it really happened, we have to bleed on paper. We have to let people in on the fact that we don't have all the answers. We have to let people into the dark places of our story. And if we don't write the real story, isn't it just a waste of paper?

YOU DON'T HAVE TO GO

I sat in my apartment alone most days, writing a book I wasn't sure anyone would ever read. I did it because I wanted to, because even if no one ever read the words I was committing to paper, I needed to write them. I didn't do it because God told me to, or because I would be sinning if I didn't. I did it because I had to, because I couldn't not. I did it because, without the fear and insecurity and excuses getting in my way, there was nothing stopping me anymore.

This time there was no bartering with God, no conditions under which I would write or wouldn't. I didn't tell Him, "If I get a book deal, then I'll keep writing," or, "If I get a full-time writing job, then I'll do it." I didn't even tell Him He had to pay my bills, or give me a sign. I just did it. I just started writing and decided I wouldn't quit writing until it was finished. I did it because I wanted to, because it was the thing that got me out of bed most mornings.

It's funny how the more responsibility you take for your actions, the more fun life becomes. You would think it would be the opposite, wouldn't it? I mean, we spend most of our lives trying to pass off the responsibility and the blame to somebody else. But the more responsibility we try to give away, the more miserable we become. We try to blame God, or other people, for our miserable circumstances, but then our circumstances just become more miserable. The longer we play the victim, the more we believe we really are one.

As I wrote, I thought about how I almost didn't go on the trip. I thought about the words Sharaya told me that day in the coffee shop. She said, "You don't have to go. But if you don't, you'll regret

246 | packing light

it," and for the first time since she said them so many months ago, I realized what she meant. It was so simple. I don't know how I had missed it before. I had always focused on the second part, but it was the first part that struck me now. *You don't have to go.*

There were so many times on the trip I thought I had been forced to go. I remembered Washington, DC, dragging my feet to all the stupid monuments, angry that I was doing this whole thing without Ben. It was so easy to blame it on Sharaya. She had convinced me to come. Hadn't she? Or maybe God had.

I remembered her words in a commanding tone, the way I imagine God when He talks to me. "If you don't do it the right way, you'll be sorry," she had said, like she was expressing preemptive disappointment, just waiting for me to do it wrong. When things got hard, it was a toss-up between believing I had done it wrong and this was my punishment, or that this was all God's fault. "This is the right way to do it," I pictured God saying. "You think it's hard? Suck it up." It wasn't until later I realized Sharaya didn't make me do anything. Neither did God. I did it all by myself.

Sharaya's message to me in the coffee shop that day, the day I decided I'd go on the trip, is one that I'll take with me forever, and I'll pass it on to you as well.

You don't have to go. You can stay home. It's up to you. But if you let fear stop you from doing what you really want to do, you'll regret that forever.

The morning I woke up and told Sharaya I was all in, I thought I was being obedient to God's will. I think we do this often as Christians, and I think it's a misunderstanding of God's character. God wasn't telling me what to do. He was just helping me to see what I actually wanted. He was saying, "Here's permission to want what you want, regardless of what anyone else thinks. Here's permission to be the woman I created you to be. You think you don't have the resources, but you do. I will provide them. You think you aren't strong enough to face the obstacles, but you are. I'll be with you the whole time. Here's permission to live your life, not dictated by fear of what might happen. Go ahead, jump off the waterfall."

God didn't make me go on the road trip with Sharaya in the same way He didn't make the "rich young ruler" sell his possessions. He's not making you do anything you don't want to do, either. He's doesn't control us like that. But He is inviting you. He is giving you a choice. Some of us choose to walk away, like the "rich young ruler," and God is not mad at us about that. He might be sad, and come to think of it, we might be sad too. We should all be sad when we miss out on the fullness of life God has to offer us.

Something happens when we stop seeing God as a controlling God who tells us what we have to do and what we can't do. We stop feeling so much anger toward Him. Because if God made me go on the trip, than each of the difficulties I experienced along the way were His fault. He has to take responsibility for them, and when He doesn't, I feel frustrated and angry. *Why didn't things turn out the way I hoped, God? Why didn't I get what I wanted out of this?* I start to feel like God didn't return His promise when the truth is, God never promised me anything. The only thing He promised was that He would be with me, and that none of it would be wasted.

The one thing I wanted was to not be alone, when the truth was He was with me all along.

The beautiful thing about looking at God this way is that we haven't messed anything up. Our life is not ruined. We're not being punished. We're not doing it wrong. God isn't mad at us; He's just waiting for us to wake up, to take responsibility, and to start living life with Him. He's waiting for us to do something beautiful, something courageous, something totally out of the ordinary.

Your whole life is an invitation. God isn't going to tell you the "right" answer or force you in a certain direction, because if He did, He would only be stealing the joy that comes when you pick yourself. You'll face obstacles along the way, like we did. There will be breakdowns and sickness, and losses you can't imagine before you start. But God isn't punishing you. He's on your side. He's never left you. He'll be with you the whole way.

Your life is waiting. But your arms are full of stuff. We all have baggage of one kind or another. Will you put yours down to go on a trip? Trust me—you won't come home the same.

Afterword

the way you pack

WHEN YOU GO ON a trip, you choose your luggage carefully, based on its size and durability. If you're going on a hiking trip, you choose a bag that's just big enough to fit the bare necessities. You'll need a bag that can stand up to the natural elements and challenges of hiking, one that can take the sweat and the scraping of tree bark and being thrown down in the dirt for a break to get some water. For a trip to Disney World, you find a big suitcase—one that has a stand-out color to add to the whimsy, and big enough to fit all the souvenirs you'll buy.

And then you begin packing your belongings, thinking carefully about where you're going, what you think you'll experience, and who you'll meet. You pack an extra pair of wool socks, a waterproof jacket in case it rains, a jacket for when dusk falls at Universal Studios. You only bring the things with you that are most important. You only have so much space.

And when you're done you have a tiny little container (tiny in comparison to what you've left behind, even if it is quite big) of you that you bring along. If something were to happen to you, and someone were to find your luggage, they would open it and carefully sort through your belongings. The things they find would tell a story—your story—of where you were going, who you were, and what really mattered. What would that story look like?

We pack differently for different trips. We take all kinds of things into consideration. How long will we be gone? What is our destination? What is the purpose of going? But no matter the variables, you can't take everything with you. You don't take stiletto heels with you camping (and even if you did, what would you do with them?). You don't take your painting clothes with you on a business trip. You don't need those things with you. You probably don't even want them. They would just weigh you down. It's better to leave them behind.

Even when you move to a new place, you make these kinds of value judgements. You might pack up your whole house, but you also take loads of "stuff" to Goodwill and the dump. You wave goodbye to your favorite hangouts and restaurants, neighborhood quirks, and community of friends—all the things you can't take with you.

This all seems so obvious, doesn't it?

So then why are so many of us so bad at packing?

Men pack differently than women. A businessman packs differently than a Bohemian. A mother packs differently than a single woman. But this fact remains: What you pack says something about who you are.

Try to imagine yourself packing in a hurry. What would you take? What if you didn't know when you would be back? What if you could only pack the trunk and backseat of your car? What if all you were allowed was one small box? What would you put in that box? What would you do if something happened to that box?

What would you miss the most? Why do those things matter to you so much?

I have this recurring nightmare about luggage. Even though it comes in different forms depending on the occasion, it goes something like this: I am on a trip, and my luggage has been lost. Maybe it fell out of the back of a moving vehicle, so that my things are sent careening all over the highway. This version happens in slow motion, with dramatic music playing in the background. I turn, contorting to resist my seat belt, looking out the back window of the vehicle and watching the suitcase tumble, over and over, until every last item has fallen out. In another version the airline lost my luggage, and I am sent on a wild goose chase to find it. First, I'm told a restaurant owner has it, but the restaurant is closed. Then a kind patron of the restaurant offers to show me to the owner's house. It's midnight, and I'm knocking on this stranger's door, looking for a way inside. You get the picture.

Ultimately, I wake up without finding my luggage, wondering why my subconscious finds this matter so important as to torture me over it night after night.

What's the big deal about our stuff?

Like the "rich young ruler," I think we are a people of great wealth. You might not agree, but it's true. If you drive a car or have access to transportation, you have great wealth. If you own a computer, or a smartphone, or a phone at all, you are a person of great wealth. If you are holding this book in your hands (even if it's from a library), you are a person of means. If you have access to education (formal or otherwise), you are rich. You are a person of many possessions, some tangible and some intangible.

With such wealth at your fingertips, you have expectations about what your life is supposed to look like. Some of them you've imposed on yourself; others you've inherited from someone else.

You have wants, desires, needs, and ideas. These are all things you "pack" with you for the journey. You might not even know you're carrying them, but they're in there. You're walking around with a heavy suitcase.

What if the concept of baggage is cliché for a reason? Like renowned travel guide Rick Steves says, no traveler brags that, each time she goes on a trip, she brings more stuff with her. No. She realizes that the last time she went, she didn't wear half of what she packed, that the hotel provided all of the amenities she needed, and she remembers how uncomfortable it was to lug all of those bags from the airport to the shuttle to her destination.

Are you packing light?

If your life was a trip and you could only bring so much with you, what would you bring? What would you be willing to leave behind? Are there things, thoughts, and ideas you are so attached to that they're preventing you from getting anywhere? What are they? What would happen if you released your tight grip on those things for just a minute? Maybe, just maybe, you would get to see what is *out there*. Maybe you would get to go on a trip.

PASS IT ON

Packing Light is about learning to live life with less baggage, and that includes letting go of things like books (sometimes). Share this book with a friend and keep a running list of the people in your life who are packing light. Sign your name and the date below before passing this book along.

Allison Vesterfelt
Packing Light

DATE	ISSUED TO

MOODY
PUBLISHERS
www.MoodyPublishers.com

moody
collective

Moody Collective brings words of life to a generation seeking deeper faith. We are a part of Moody Publishers, representing this next generation of followers of Christ through books, blogs, essays, and more.

We seek to know, love, and serve the millennial generation with grace and humility. Each of our books is intended to challenge and encourage our readers as they pursue God. To learn more, visit our website, www.moodycollective.com.

LIFE AFTER ART

978-0-8024-0739-9

For most adults, the art room is a memory from long-lost childhood school days. Art class probably did not mean much more than smearing crayons and paint onto construction paper-with no real value to an adult who is dealing with the pressures of relationships, careers, finances, and raising a family.

Even with these external pressures, the biggest concern adults often face is the spiritual crisis of self-value. We fear unmet ambitions. We fear that our lives have little meaning, purpose, or value. We fear that God has a plan for us, but we're missing it. These fears prevent us from leading the productive, contented, joy-filled lives that God created us to live.

also available as an ebook

MOODY
PUBLISHERS
www.MoodyPublishers.com

THE IN-BETWEEN

978-0-8024-0724-5

We're an "instant gratification" generation, but the trouble is, most change happens gradually.

Most of us spend our lives searching and longing for something more than what is in front of us. Whether it's traveling abroad or chasing cheap (or expensive) thrills, we're all looking for medicine to satisfy our restlessness. And, so often, we're looking in the wrong place.

The In-Between is a call to accept the importance that waiting plays in our lives. Can we embrace the extraordinary nature of the ordinary and enjoy the daily mundane-what lies in between the "major" moments?

also available as an ebook

MOODY
PUBLISHERS

www.MoodyPublishers.com